The Learning Curve

Navigating the Road to High School Success

Alice Giarrusso

ISBN: 978-0-578-19775-3 (sc)
ISBN: 978-0-578-19789-0 (e)

Library of Congress Control Number: 2018902025

Rev. date: 06/07/2018

Learning Curve Publications
Alice Renee Giarrusso

Contents

This book is dedicated to my mom and dad.
I could not have been more blessed than to have them for my parents.

And to my sons, Mark and Joseph,
who own my heart.

PART I
Welcome to The Learning Curve

Every fall, with the approaching cold weather, the monarch butterflies of Canada embark upon a two thousand–mile journey that takes them to parts of Southern California and Mexico, sometimes to the very same tree that once housed their ancestors. Across the prairies they fly over, the tumbleweed blows. With no root system to hold it fast and at the whim of every gust of wind, the tumbleweed's course, unlike the monarch's, is unpredictable.

Monarch butterfly or tumbleweed? Where are you heading?

Without thinking about the path we would like to take in high school or about where we want to be when we graduate, we run the risk of being like the tumbleweed—at the whim of circumstance and outside forces. The days, weeks, and even years may pass, leaving us to wonder if our time was spent wisely.

The Learning Curve is a road map for navigating your way through the intricate twists and turns of high school, leading you to the place you would like to be. It creates a mind-set for success while developing practical skills for achieving that success. Like a road map and the monarch butterfly, *The Learning Curve* requires that you think about where you are now, where you'd like to be in the future, and how you intend to get there. Let's begin.

1

Who Is the Author of Your Life Story?

Wherever you are in your educational journey, or your life's journey for that matter, *you* are in the driver's seat. Your future is in *your* hands. The book of your life has yet to be written, and it is *yours* to write. It is now time to write the chapter of your life that has to do with high school.

✎ **How will you write it, and what will it include?**

✎ **Do you know how you want this chapter to end?**

As a writer gives prior thought to the things he or she wants to write, you too can give prior thought to how you want your high school chapter to read. One way to do this is to think about what is important to you and what you hope to achieve. Your next step is to formulate goals for making those dreams a reality.

Let's start with a visualization activity.

Visualization Activity

Here and Now

1. What are your hopes and dreams for your high school years?

   _____

   _____

   _____

2. What are your plans for making those hopes and dreams become reality?

   _____

   _____

   _____

3. What obstacles do you anticipate encountering?

   _____

   _____

   _____

4. How do you envision yourself overcoming those obstacles?

   _____

   _____

   _____

Fast-Forward to Graduation Day

Imagine now it is your graduation day. Your high school years have flown by. You're in your graduation cap and gown, standing alongside your classmates. A major chapter in your life is coming to a close, but your experiences will remain with you forever. As you imagine yourself looking back on your high school experience, imagine yourself looking back from a position of achievement and contentment. Essentially, you have created a story of success, a chapter in your life with a happy ending.

1. What was your life like in high school?

    _____

    _____

    _____

    _____

2. What were your major accomplishments?

    _____

    _____

    _____

    _____

3. How are you feeling right now, and why are you feeling that way?

    _____

    _____

    _____

    _____

4. What is the next step in your life? Did your performance in high school help you get to this next step?

_____

_____

_____

_____

2

The Four Key Elements
of School Success

By imagining these four years, you have created the outline of a story you would like to live. So how do you go about actually living that story and making those dreams a reality?

How do you make your dreams for success a reality?

Throughout this book, I will be referring to four key elements that I believe school success is based on. They are as follows.

The Four Key Elements of School Success

1. Assign value to what you are doing.

2. Intend to succeed. Plan to do well.

3. Be your own cheerleader.

4. Practice. Practice. Practice.

Element 1—Assign Value to What You Are Doing

Ask yourself these questions: Why is what I'm learning important? Why is it important to do well?

You keep hearing it from everyone—school is important, and you need to do well. But what exactly do those words mean?

Why is it important to do well? You may think, *I can learn what I need later on. I know people who didn't do well in high school and have succeeded afterward.* A few may have, but you can't count on that.

Knowing why it is important to do well is the first step on the path to school success. This is explained in what I refer to as The Three Big Reasons to Do Well.

The Three Big Reasons to Do Well

Reason 1—*You Get to Take All You Learn with You*

The beautiful thing about learning is that no one can take it away from you.

—B. B. King

Whatever you learn while you are in school is yours to keep. You never have to give it back, and it can never be taken from you. The knowledge you obtain and the skills you develop become an integral and invaluable part of the person you are. What you learn will serve to make you stronger, more capable, and more ready for the world.

Your future has yet to unfold, so enriching yourself with knowledge and skills is your best preparation for what lies ahead.

I will study and get ready and someday my chance will come.

—Abraham Lincoln

Reason 2—*It Increases Your Options and Makes You More Marketable*

Let's face it: the more you know, the more of an asset you will be. Your performance in high school is, for better or worse, ascertained by your grade point average or GPA. Every point higher on your GPA will give you more options when applying for college. You are not competing against others as much as you are competing against yourself. A 2.8 is better than at 2.7, a 3.5 is better than a 3.4, and so forth. Each point higher increases your marketability.

Your grades are a representation of your time spent in school. To outsiders, admissions officers, or potential employers, they represent not only knowledge acquired in specific courses but also potential success rate. Course grades represent a certain level of skill mastery. Success in a class represents the meeting of deadlines, the completion of specific tasks, and the ability to meet requirements and expectations.

What you do today, this week, and this year in school is directly related to your future. Taking the evening off and getting a zero on an assignment will affect you. Sure, maybe you can make up that zero, but the time making it up could have been spent moving forward instead of just catching up. Frittering your time away instead of putting in a little extra study time when you know you need it will create situations that work against you and your goals.

So what you do today, this week, and this year is absolutely directly related to your future. Take a look at the following example of a conversation I once had with a student.

> Me—So how's everything going?
> Student—Good, except I just got a zero on my history homework.
> Me—Yikes, what happened?
> Student—Well, I didn't do it.
> Me—Why?
> Student—I was tired, so I went to bed.
> Me—You were tired, so you went to bed. Was it really late?
> Student—Not really, it was nine thirty.
> Me—So how much time do you think you needed to complete that assignment?
> Student—I don't know, no more than twenty minutes.
> Me—Well, did you have a big test in another subject that you really wanted to be rested for?
> Student—No.
> Me—Did you have a big game that you had to be your best for?
> Student—No.
> Me—Hmmm ... so you went to bed instead of staying up an extra twenty minutes and took a zero instead?
> Student—Yeah ...
> Me—What am I actually saying to you here?
> Student—I get it. Why didn't I just stay up those extra twenty minutes and finish my work?

Me—Or what else?

Student—I could have started earlier and gotten it done that way too.

Be mindful of the little decisions you make on a daily basis that will either build or erode your GPA. In the course of your year, you are going to encounter things that are beyond your control—a test grade that got out of hand, an assignment you misunderstood, or a personal situation that comes up. These things are bound to happen occasionally. Don't add to these mishaps by *giving* your success away. Taking a zero when you absolutely did not need to creates a situation where you are using energy to catch up instead of moving ahead.

Reason 3—*You're Practicing the Skills You Need to Be Successful in School and Beyond*

High school is not only your learning time for facts and information but also a time for practicing skills! Along with the subject matter, there exists in school a "hidden" curriculum that will prove equally important. Failure in this hidden curriculum will make success elsewhere extremely difficult. The hidden curriculum includes the practice and development of essential lifelong skills necessary for survival and success. High school affords you a place to practice these skills as you work toward a lifetime of competency. These skills include the following:

Time Management

Can I juggle all that I need to do successfully?

Can I manage sports, clubs, jobs, *and* my academic responsibilities?

Do I plan how to use my time and follow through with those plans?

A study from the 1990s followed students from high school through college and tested them on their time-management skills. It came as no surprise that students with better time-management skills performed better in the classroom than peers with poor management skills. But what was particularly noteworthy was that students with strong time-management skills also outperformed peers in the classroom who had higher SAT scores but weaker time-management skills, supporting the idea that these skills play a crucial role in school success (Britton and Tesser 1991).

Organizational Skills

Can I quickly find what I am looking for?

Am I overwhelmed by papers and miscellaneous clutter?

Do I have an effective system in place that addresses the organization of all the books, notebooks, papers, and other school-related paraphernalia I have?

What do my desk, backpack, and locker look like?

Task Initiation

Do I begin my projects early enough to ensure quality work?

Is it hard for me to get started? What stops me?

Task Completion

Do I start things and not finish?

Do I finish tasks on time?

Am I always looking for an extension?

Am I often making excuses?

Problem solving

Can I strategize and develop plans for addressing problems that come my way?

Do I foresee problems that might arise?

Goal Setting

Have I given thought to my goals?

What do I want my final product to look like?

Am I keeping track of my progress along the way to best ensure I get there?

Self-Advocacy

What resources can I use to help me overcome obstacles and achieve my goals?

How can I best express myself and my needs in a positive way to those who are in a position to help me?

The skills mentioned above are just some of the skills you practice and develop in high school to help ensure your success later on in college, in the workforce, and in all areas of your life.

High school affords you the opportunity to practice and fine-tune these skills in a relatively safe environment, rather than the harsher, more competitive environment of college and the adult workplace.

The Three Big Reasons to Do Well are listed below. Write next to each one what it means to you.

You Get to Take What You Learn with You

_____

_____

_____

It Increases Your Options and Makes You More Marketable

_____

_____

_____

You're Practicing the Skills You Need to Be Successful

_____

_____

_____

Element 2—Intend to Succeed—Plan to Do Well

The word *intentional* refers to doing something on purpose. It is something done deliberately and consciously. It is thought out and preplanned. When you intend to succeed, you strategize and plan for success, and most importantly, you believe in the possibility of attaining success.

Students who intend to succeed, regardless of the obstacles they may encounter, view challenges and failures as learning opportunities that will better prepare them for the future. They work to adapt to changing conditions and seek to continually build on their knowledge base. They believe in their ability to grow and develop, even when it is difficult. Thinking of the word *intentional* in this regard makes it easy to see why being intentional is an essential quality for a successful student to have.

> Success doesn't just happen.
> It is hard work.
> It requires resilience.
> It is intentional.

—Alice Giarrusso

Intention can best be explained by the following story.

The Number 34 Syracuse Lacrosse Jersey

Years ago, a sixth-grade boy studiously worked on his homework. His task was to create a collage that best represented who he was—his interests, his aspirations, his dreams. When completed, his collage pictured a large lacrosse jersey with "Syracuse" boldly written across the top and the number 34 emblazoned in orange. Playing lacrosse for Syracuse University—the holder of more national championship titles in lacrosse than any other school—was the fantasy of every young lacrosse player he knew, on par with playing for the Yankees for baseball players or in the NHL for aspiring hockey players.

Six years later, this young man stood at his high school graduation. Underneath his cap and gown, he wore a Syracuse lacrosse T-shirt, even though he would soon be attending a different school. While he had realized his dream of playing Division 1 lacrosse, it was not at Syracuse. At the conclusion of his freshman year in college, after working hard for excellent grades, he applied and transferred to Syracuse, giving up an athletic scholarship along with a place on a college team. The following year he made the Syracuse lacrosse team as a walk-on, and was assigned the number fifty-one. You might think the story ended happily there, but there was more. During his years on the team, he was assigned other numbers—first fifty-one and then forty-eight. A picture of the team's seniors, taken together at their last game, shows this determined young man proudly standing with his teammates in his lacrosse jersey, with Syracuse boldly written across the top and the number 34 emblazoned in orange.

It wasn't until several years after his graduation that his mother (that's me!) found the sixth-grade collage stored safely away in the attic. Over the years, I had completely forgotten about it. At the time that he created it, the collage, while nice, held little exceptional meaning for me. But on that day in the attic, fourteen years later, as I reflected on his journey, that collage brought this young man's mother to tears.

How does this story relate to the quote above, "Success doesn't just happen. It is hard work. It requires resilience. It is intentional"?

_____

_____

_____

_____

It all started with a dream, an *intention*, a goal. But it became reality by keeping an eye on the final destination, even if the path taken to get there was not direct. People don't accidentally succeed and achieve their goals. They have intention, they overcome obstacles, and they persevere. Think of the great success stories you know. What did they do to get where they are?

Success *Is* Intentional

Activity

Visualize the Path to School Success

On the lines below, describe the things you will do to achieve your goal of high school success.

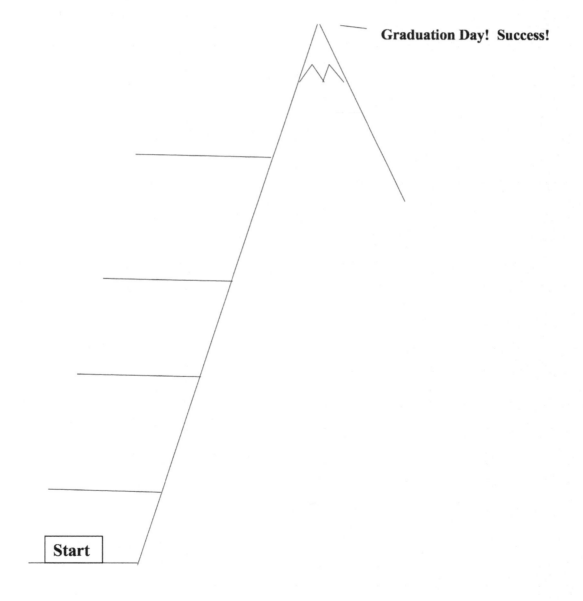

Graduation Day! Success!

Start

Element 3—Be Your Own Cheerleader

As you go through high school and life in general, be aware of your inner voice and what it is saying to you. Is it supporting and encouraging you with positive statements like: "You can do this," and "Sure it's hard, but you've done hard things before," or is it working against you with comments like, "This is too hard. Give up, and go home"?

Your inner voice, though silent to the rest of the world, may be the most powerful ally you will ever have, or conversely, it may be a destructive foe. It can be your greatest cheerleader, spurring you on to greatness, or it can keep you from living the life you dream of.

Your inner voice does not work in isolation. It responds to what is heard and experienced. The good thing about our inner voice is that it can be talked back to and persuaded to change its mind. We can even offer it preformulated scripts when all else fails. These are things we repeatedly tell ourselves to encourage and support ourselves. Examples are:

"Every step backward just allows for a bigger running start."
"Every day is a new beginning. Take a deep breath and start again."
"All things are difficult before they are easy."

—Thomas Fuller

We can train our inner voice to work with us, instead of against us, but first we must be aware of its existence. Your inner voice influences your attitude and your ability to be resilient, both of which are enormously important not only for school success but also for success in life.

What is your inner voice saying to you right now? Is it saying, "Go for it! Be all you can be"? Think of your inner voice as a really supportive friend. What are some of the positive things you'd like to hear your inner voice say?

1. Shoot for the stars
2. dont give up
3. be yourself

Activity

Working with Your Inner Voice

Respond to each scenario with a positive, supportive inner voice—an inner voice that is on your side.

Scenario 1—It's the first day of school. You were up most of the night feeling anxious. What is your supportive inner voice saying to you?

Don't be nervous, you will do great.

_____

_____

_____

Scenario 2—You just took a chemistry test, and you know you did not do well. What would a supportive inner voice be saying?

Make sure you dont put your head down.
Work harder next time.

_____

_____

Scenario 3—Midterm exams are coming up in two weeks, and this also coincides with (pick one) the school play you are in, your driver's ed class starting up, or the semifinals for your sport. How are you going to manage it all, and what would a supportive inner voice be saying to you?

Try to manage your time, since the semi
finals are coming up make sure you are
staying healthy while you also study for
exams.

Element 4—Practice, Practice, Practice

We are what we repeatedly do. Excellence, then, is not an act but a habit.

—Will Durant, philosopher

School affords you the opportunity to continually practice all you are learning. School is first and foremost a period of growth and progression. No one expects you to arrive knowing everything and being perfect. → No one is perfect

Who you are as a student is not a fixed thing. A good student in ninth grade does not guarantee a good student in the other grades, and conversely, performing poorly in ninth grade does not make you permanently a poor student. It is easy for things to change in school, and it is all based on your effort and performance. Improvements can be made by taking a careful look at what you are doing and developing strategies for change. → you learn from mistakes.

As you learn new things, you will make changes to the things you are already doing, keeping what works, discarding what doesn't, and always modifying to make improvements. As a team continually practices to stay in shape and compete against opponents, your work will be your practice, delivering you successfully to the stage to receive your diploma on graduation day.

Academic success can be achieved by developing and practicing strong study skills, and by hard work. By academic success, I don't mean you're guaranteed to get straight As, although you might; what's important is that your time spent in school will be worthwhile, your grades will improve, and you will finish the school year ahead of where you started as a more enriched person, with much to show for your time and effort. I hope to improve as a student.

What are the things you need to practice? What do you need to do to succeed?

Check the appropriate columns—NI = Needs Improvement

Things to Practice Checklist	Yes	No	NI
Seeing the Value in What You Do	✓		
Being Your Own Cheerleader	✓		
Intending/Planning to Succeed	✓		
Being Attentive in Class	✓		
Organizing Papers and Materials	✓		
Getting Started on Work	✓		
Completing Assignments	✓		
Meeting Deadlines	✓		
Being Prepared with Materials	✓		
Completing Long-Term Assignments	✓		
Time Management	✓		
Problem Solving	✓		
Self-Advocacy	✓		
Goal Setting	✓		

PART II

The Practicalities of Doing Well: The Things You Need to Practice

3
The Tools to Be Successful

1. **The Agenda**

2. **School Websites**

3. **The Notebook System**

4. **At-Home Portable File Box**

The Agenda

Just as a surgeon needs a scalpel, a navigator needs a map, and a carpenter needs a hammer, you as a student have very specific tools that are necessary for academic success. It is in your best interest to set yourself up prior to the start of every school year, but if it is later in the year, now is a good time too!

The first essential tool is the agenda; a planner, date book, assignment book, or special place where you record assignments and due dates for work. Many schools make recommendations as to the type of agenda book that they think works best. Some schools even supply them. If an agenda is not provided or recommended, then find one that will work well for you. The most important thing to remember is that you need to *use* it. Too many students simply carry one around and never, ever use it.

Any successful person, whether a student in high school or a CEO of a large corporation, who is forced to juggle a lot of tasks and deadlines absolutely needs a place to record what he or she needs to do and when he or she needs to do it by. It is impossible to keep everything in your head. If you have up until now, that will not continue as your workload increases in amount and complexity. Eventually, probably sooner rather than later, you will overlook something important. In addition to serving as a reminder of what needs to be done, the agenda also contributes to the development of good time management and organizational skills.

Things that don't typically work as well as agendas:

- *Your memory!*
- *Little spiral assignment books with blank pages.* Pages fall out, there's no specific place to write, and you can't see a week at a glance. They're fine for jotting little reminder notes and thoughts that cross your mind but not for serious work.
- *E-calendars.* While these certainly have their place and can be used in other ways, they do not match the versatility of a physical planner, especially for students new to high school and the high school demands. That being said, if it's not broke, don't fix it! This means that if you have a reasonable system in place and it is successful, keep doing it. There are many ways to accomplish the same goal. The proof will be in the pudding, or in the grades. But if assignments aren't being handed in and deadlines are unmet, critically look at the system you are using, or not using, and make some changes.

Tips for Agenda Use

Tip 1—Never leave home without it!

Your agenda is your life raft, your parachute, your anchor, and your best friend in time of need!

Tip 2—Fill it in at the beginning of every week and update it daily.

Many teachers post their assignments on class or school websites; in fact, many schools require their teachers to do so. Log on to the designated sites at the beginning of every week with your agenda in front of you. Copy from the website every homework assignment you need for the week. Also log into the homework sites frequently during the week to see if new assignments have been given or if there are any other important announcements.

Tip 3—Take your agenda out at the beginning of every class.

Be ready for any assignments your teachers might give at the spur of the moment. You have probably realized that every teacher does not assign work the same way. Some may post it somewhere in the classroom, some might just verbally announce it, or some may use a website. Regardless of the method they use, it is your responsibility to adapt to it. You want to be ready for those on-the-fly changes or additions a teacher might make. If your agenda is ready, you can immediately write it in instead of counting on remembering it, which is risky. Also, there's always the chance that you could be inattentive or be daydreaming when the announcement is made. Simply having your agenda out in front of you will make you more likely to focus in on anything that may come up, as you have already cued your brain to the potential of an assignment coming your way. Think of a catcher holding his mitt in the ready position to better catch the pitch; having your agenda out and open makes it more likely you will "catch" assignments your teacher may unexpectedly send your way. You can also approach the teacher at the end of the class with your agenda open and confirm that you have everything written down that you need to.

Tip 4—Write in upcoming tests, quizzes, and long-term assignments.

I recommend that you write in the upcoming test or quiz on the actual test date in *red*, so it is sure to stand out. Then *plan backward* for the test or quiz by writing it in pencil or pen on the days you plan to study for it. For example, if your biology teacher assigns a chapter 2 test on Friday, you would write in red on Friday "Biology—chapter 2 test." Then you would determine how many days you need to study for this test and the days that you can do this. So if you feel you need two days to study, you might write into your assignment book on both Wednesday and Thursday nights, "Study for biology test."

Tip 5—Always take out your agenda as you begin your homework.

Referring to your agenda before starting your work will serve as a reminder of what needs to be done. Even if you think you have no homework to do, still take it out and look to be sure.

Tip 6—Use your agenda for time management and prioritizing.

Before beginning your assignments, give some thought to what tasks are most important and how long you anticipate each task to take. Then number your assignments in the order you have decided to do them. In parentheses, put how long you anticipate each assignment to take. Doing this will give you a good overview of what needs to be done and how much time you will need.

Tip 7—As you complete your nightly assignments, check them off.

This not only lets you clearly see what is left to do, but it also lends itself to a rewarding feeling of, "Ahhh … things are getting done. I've accomplished something." Things that need to be carried over to the next day should be indicated as such in the agenda book.

Tip 8—Don't Stop Using Your Agenda When You Are Successful!

This may be the most important agenda tip. Remember, continue doing what brings you success, and if using your agenda brings you success, don't mislead yourself into thinking that you can stop using it and continue to have success. Make using your agenda your default habit.

What does your agenda look like?

_____

_____

How do you use it?

_____

_____

How will you use it in the future?

_____

_____

School Websites

Many teachers and schools use a website to post homework assignments along with grades. Using this site on a regular and frequent basis will contribute to your success.

As you sit down to do your homework, log in to this site. Confirm the assignments you have been given, and check for any changes the teacher may have made.

Many of the programs used by schools today have grades in real time, meaning this site acts as a teacher's grade book. As soon as a grade is entered, the student can view it, along with the updated and current average. Checking the grade portion of the site is important for two major reasons:

1. The site informs you of any missing work you may have that you have overlooked. Perhaps you were absent and were unaware of an assignment, or perhaps you have just forgotten to hand something in.

2. It engages you and keeps you in the game. Here's what I mean. If you are involved in a competitive basketball game, I'm sure you keep your eye on the score. Being one basket behind is going to spur you on to catch up. Being three baskets ahead is going to make you want to hang on to your lead and encourage you to keep playing hard. Knowing where you stand engages and motivates you.

Does your school have a website for students?

_____

What is it?

_____

Do you know your log in information and how to access it?

_____

The Notebook System

What do you actually bring into the classroom with you to take notes, to store handouts the teacher may give you, and to put ingoing and outgoing homework in? In this day and age, many students use technology for their note-taking and for submitting assignments online. While schools may be using less paper, there still exists a need for an organized system of storing written information for each class. Unless your school is directing you toward one particular system, this decision will be up to you. How you decide to organize yourself does not have to be a permanent commitment. If it is working, keep it; if it isn't, it's time for a change.

There are many different ways to address the notebook situation. I'd like to share with you some systems that did not work for the particular students who chose them. Think about how you would improve each situation.

Situation 1 –

One day in mid-October, I met with a freshman I had never met with before. He walked into my office, not only with a backpack but also a large plastic bag. Both the backpack and the bag looked to be bursting at the seams. As he exasperatedly ran his hand through his hair, he looked at me and said, "I need help!"

He and his mom had put a lot of thought into getting him ready for high school. They shopped in August in preparation for the start of school and had designed a system that they thought would be fail-proof. For each of his six school subjects, he would have three separate things: a one-inch three-ring binder, a spiral notebook, and a pocket folder for handouts. Each class would be in a different color; for example, a green binder, green spiral notebook, and green pocket folder, would be for biology, while a blue binder, blue spiral notebook, and blue pocket folder would be for math, and so on. They designed this particular system because they both agreed that this young man was organizationally challenged. However, as you can imagine, carrying around eighteen different things, and deciding what to use them for, was creating its own kind of nightmare. The only thing that would have been worse for this boy is if all eighteen things were in the same color, which I have also seen!

Situation 2 –

Well into the school year, a harried-looking sophomore burst into my office, collapsed into a chair, and declared, "I'm a mess! I can't find anything, and I can't stand it!" When I asked him to show me what was going on, his problem became clear to me and also to him. He pulled out a large three-ring binder that had at least four times the amount of papers jammed into it than it could possibly hold. Some things were inside the rings—mostly blank, lined paper—but most things were jammed between countless other papers at odd angles, so that the edges of the papers became torn and ragged. None of the papers were separated according to subject or organized according to date. He was carrying around things he really needed but hadn't been able to find, things he no longer needed, and things he never needed, as well as numerous assignments he had received zeroes on because he couldn't locate them. He also had jammed in the bottom of his backpack another hundred or so papers that had just been put in there, either in class or at home, with the fleeting thought of putting them where they belonged later.

Situation 3 –

Another time, a top-achieving student came to see me because he often missed deadlines and misplaced his work. When I inquired as to how he organized himself and asked to see his notebook or notebooks, he looked at me with an odd smile. "I don't use a notebook," he said.

When I asked what did he use, he responded with, "Nothing." My incredulity could not be masked, as I know my eyes became wider and wider! "So, show me what you've got in that backpack," I said. Out came his laptop, with dozens of papers between the lid and keyboard, textbooks with papers folded and stuffed throughout, and one pocket folder that contained about two hundred papers that, once put in there, were never glanced at again. A look inside his backpack revealed more loose papers.

"Time to get to work," I said.

There are many different ways that students successfully organize themselves. The important thing is to have a system that's working for you. Organization is a thoughtful, reflective process. As a situation changes, people who are generally well-organized make changes in their methods to better meet the situation and continue to be successful.

Many students successfully maintain separate binders for each subject, utilize spiral notebooks, or have other methods for organizing the materials they receive in class and the notes that they take. It is always easy to see if a system is working. How are your grades? Can you find things quickly? The proof is always in the results.

Regardless of the system you have in place, if you are going to school unprepared, have difficulty finding your papers, and/or are disorganized with papers folded and stuffed in your books, book bag, and locker, then your system needs an overhaul. Knowing how to manage all the papers you will accumulate daily is essential.

One system that I recommend that has been enormously successful involves building upon the three-ring binder and includes the following:

- One or more three-ring binder(s)

  o One inch if it is for a single subject

  o One and a half inches if you are combining two or more subjects in a binder

- Pocket notebook dividers

- An at-home portable file box.

- A quality three-ring hole puncher

Here's how it works.

1. As long as your teachers are not requiring a separate binder for their particular subject, combine subjects in as few three-ring binders as possible, perhaps even a single binder. Select one that has pockets on the inside covers for specific papers that may not belong anywhere else, like permission slips and parent notices.

2. Purchase dividers for each subject, but not just any dividers. Purchase sturdy plastic ones that have their own pockets. These pockets are specifically for things that are handed out and being assigned that day. When you go home, you open your binder sections, see the work that needs to be done, and do it. When it is completed, it goes right back in the same spot and is where you will find it the next day when it is time to hand it in.

3. Behind each divider, place loose-leaf paper for note-taking, alleviating the need for a spiral notebook. Any handouts given in class, or papers that have been handed back to you, should be hole punched and placed in that particular subject area. A place for everything and everything in its place, as the saying goes.

4. At home, keep a three-hole punch so that you can punch holes in handouts your teachers have given you and then put them in the correct section of your binder.

Okay, so at this point you're saying, "That will absolutely not work for me because I have way too many papers and my binder will split open." This is where the at-home portable file box comes into play. I recommend at least once a week, (a Sunday evening before the start of the new week works well) that you sit down with your backpack, your binder, your portable file box, and a trash basket. You can even do this while watching TV. Use this time to organize your backpack and binder to see what papers can be discarded. See what papers need to be saved but don't necessarily need to be carried around. These might include past quizzes and tests, study guides, vocabulary lists, homework assignments you might want to refer to or save, or essays you've written that have been graded and returned. Many things really should be saved, as in many schools, there are midterm exams and finals, and it can be advantageous to have these things to refer to.

If you want to save these papers but do not want to carry them around, they go into your at-home file box. So, what is that exactly?

The At-Home Portable File Box

The at-home portable file box can be purchased inexpensively from a place like Walmart or Staples. They are typically under twelve dollars and are quite durable. Purchase hanging files, one for each academic subject and for anything else you might want a folder for. Label each file English, math, science, etc., and place the papers you wish to save in each file. This way your notebook will not become too overcrowded and disorganized, and you will always know where your important papers are.

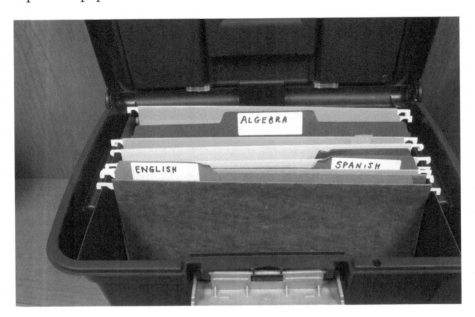

My own sons got so used to this method of organization that they also took a file box with them to college to help keep them organized there.

The basic tools for success are listed below. Please jot down any notes or thoughts you have about each item and how you see yourself using them.

1. The Agenda

_____

_____

_____

2. School Websites

_____

_____

3. The Notebook System

4. At-Home Portable File Box

At this point you've given thought to why you want to do well, and you have your basic tools in place, but what else do you need to do? A huge part of your success as a student can be ascribed to what goes on in the classroom and how you appear in the classroom.

What does a successful student look like in the classroom?

4

Success inside the Classroom

What Do You Look Like in the Classroom?

What is your impression of these students?

_____

_____

_____

_____

What do you think their teacher is thinking of them?

_____

_____

_____

_____

What do you think is necessary for success in the classroom?

_____

_____

_____

You and Your Teacher

To get an idea of what your teachers may be thinking of you, ask yourself the following questions:

Am I prepared? Do I bring with me everything I need for class, including homework, books, paper, writing utensils, and other required materials?

Am I on time and ready to learn? Do I arrive to class before the teacher begins teaching? Do I sit down and take out all necessary materials right away?

Am I attentive? Am I focused on the teacher, looking and listening to him or her? Do I make eye contact with the teacher when he/she looks my way?

Is my demeanor pleasant? Am I the sort of student I would want in my class if I were the teacher? Does my attitude and behavior add or detract from the learning environment?

Am I involved? Do I respond to questions the teacher asks the class? Do I raise my hand when I have a question? Do I actively contribute to group work?

Y=Yes, N=No, NI=Needs Improvement

Classes (write in subject)	First	Second	Third	Fourth	Fifth	Sixth	Seventh
Am I Prepared?							
Am I On Time?							
Am I Attentive?							
Am I Involved?							
Am I Pleasant?							

The impression you make on your teachers *does* matter, and it is also something that is within your control. Being prepared for class with assignments, arriving on time ready to work and attend, and contributing pleasantly to the classroom atmosphere are ways you not only ensure your own success but also contribute to the success of everyone else in your classroom. Your teachers have an important task at hand. Their job is to give you something valuable in exchange for your time. As they are attempting to accomplish this goal, you will either be an asset or a hindrance. Which do you want to be? Students who support teachers by fulfilling their roles as active, engaged, responsible students stand to gain valuable skills and knowledge in exchange for the years spent in school.

Occasionally you may come across a teacher or subject that you feel is not a particularly good match for you. During my many years as a middle school teacher, I would attend parent conferences where the parents would occasionally suggest that the reason their child wasn't doing well in a particular class was because they either didn't enjoy the subject matter or the teacher. One of the things I always said in response to this was that throughout middle school, high school, college, and beyond, students will have many teachers and numerous courses at one time. They are bound to feel differently about their teachers as they will have differing teaching styles and personalities. One teacher may become a "favorite" while another may become the "least favorite." It is also natural for them to feel more drawn to certain subject matter than others. However, that is not a reason to shut down or to do poorly. You are spending time in class, and you might as well get something out of it. Besides learning content in school, students also are learning and practicing many skills. In this case, students have an opportunity to practice the powerful skill of adaptability, so that even if a situation is not ideal, you can still be successful. Also, having an open mind toward a person or a subject might yield some very surprising results.

Up until now, how do you think your teachers have viewed you in the classroom?

_____

_____

How do you want your teachers to view you this year in the classroom?

_____

_____

There are many components to success in the classroom, some you may have already thought of and others that may not seem as obvious. Let's start with the often-overlooked basics.

Be Physically Prepared to Learn 💪

The first step to success in the classroom involves being physically prepared to learn. Being physically prepared to learn addresses your physiological needs. A living organism takes care of survival needs and general health before anything else. Optimum learning can occur when a student is well-nourished, well-rested, and fit. Being physically prepared to learn is closely tied to Key Element 2—Intend to Succeed, Plan to Do Well—because it allows you to be at an optimum state for learning.

How does one "physically prepare" oneself for learning?

Physical Requirement 1. Nutrition—Learning takes energy. 🍌

Just as a running car requires gasoline, a working brain requires fuel. This is the rationale behind the free breakfast programs in schools around the nation. Students who do not get an adequate breakfast at home are eligible to receive breakfast at school. Otherwise, what's the point? A hungry person is not able to concentrate on learning. The body takes care of the survival essentials first, and as important as learning is, it is secondary to meeting an organism's energy requirements. Breakfast (fuel) will make a difference on student performance in the classroom.

That being said, there are students who do not eat breakfast for various reasons. Time may be a factor, or they might not want to eat first thing in the morning, but the importance of breakfast still needs to be addressed.

How can you meet the energy demands of your body and brain and not have a traditional breakfast?

I suggest what I refer to as a grab-and-go. While this requires a little forethought and planning, it is incredibly easy and accomplishes its goal. A grab-and-go is exactly what it sounds like.

What can I grab and take with me? Here are some examples: juice boxes, water bottles, energy drinks, cheese sticks, granola bars, breakfast bars, protein bars, bananas, fruit, fruit cups, nuts, hard-boiled eggs, yogurts. Scan the grocery store aisles for additional ideas.

Also, please note that some students may eat breakfast at home, but that might be as early as 6:00 a.m. Lunch may not be until noon or later, and that is just too long to go without an energy boost. The ideas listed above are also easy and suitable for a midmorning snack.

Physical Requirement 2. Sufficient Sleep—When you sleep well, you think well. You have to be well rested to be at your best in the classroom. 🖚

Just as your body requires energy for learning, it also requires rest to repair and restore itself. Repeated studies say that the average teenager requires between eight and ten hours of sleep. Studies indicate that when students get less sleep one week than another, their grades decline. Being tired in school negatively impacts your concentration and your ability to learn. Adequate sleep has also been linked to improved memory and problem-solving abilities.

Due to busy schedules and various demands, getting enough sleep on a regular basis may be a challenge. Sleep needs to be planned for and budgeted into your busy schedule. Sleep time needs to be protected. That being said, it still may be difficult to get the amount of sleep you need all the time. The upside of this is that sleep can be banked. Not a lot of it, and not all the time, but occasionally. That is, if you are running a slight deficit one night, you can catch up the next and rebound. That is why it is actually a good idea for you to sleep late on the weekends if you can. You're catching up and replenishing your sleep account.

Physical Requirement 3. Exercise—The final part of getting your physical self ready to learn. 🍸

A well-tuned machine runs better than an unused, rusty one, and the same can be said for your body. An exercised body will sleep better at night, will be better able to meet the demands of sitting in the classroom, and will circulate oxygen throughout your body and brain more efficiently, thereby helping to meet the needs of your brain as it learns. Exercise has been found to stimulate brain cell growth and increase connections between cells, greatly facilitating learning. Studies have repeatedly shown the benefits exercise can have on memory retention, concentration, mood, sleep, and general health.

If you are currently involved in a sport, that may address your fitness needs, but if you are not involved in sports or if it's off-season, being mindful of your activity level is important. Getting involved in an hour of exercise daily, or as often as possible, is optimum. This can be a pick-up game of basketball, jogging, tennis, dance, yoga, exercise classes, and a variety of other activities. When that is not possible, whatever you may be able to do is beneficial; the important thing is to add movement to your life.

Certain activities may be easier to accommodate into your particular schedule than others. Walking, riding a bicycle, stretching, and jumping rope are just some ideas of activities that can be done on the spur of the moment and without prior planning. For those of you with dogs, both you and your dog can benefit greatly from the fresh air and exercise of going for a walk.

In addition to the benefits of exercise on your body and mind, exercise has also been shown to increase self-esteem and to boost the mood. To quote Hippocrates, "All people in a bad mood should go for a walk, and if it does not improve, walk again."

In summary, bringing the best *you* into the classroom means attending to the physiological needs of eating properly, getting adequate sleep, and finding time to exercise. This is not only important so you can *learn* effectively and efficiently, but also so you *live* effectively and efficiently.

Activities

Sleep Tracker: For one week, without making any conscious changes, log how much sleep you get each night and how you feel the next day, using this scale.

1—Very Tired 2—A Little Tired 3—Good 4—Well Rested and Energetic

Day	Hours	Score
Sunday		
Monday		
Tuesday		
Wednesday		
Thursday		
Friday		
Saturday		

What did you notice about your sleep patterns?

_____

_____

_____

_____

What changes, if any, will you make in your life to get adequate sleep?

_____

_____

_____

_____

Activity Tracker: What are some ways you are currently getting movement and exercise in your day?

1. _____

2. _____

3. _____

How can you bring more movement and exercise into your day?

1. _____

2. _____

3. _____

Food /Energy Tracker: For one week, without making any conscious changes, monitor your food intake in relation to energy and attention. Record yes or no for breakfast and midmorning snack, and then use an adjective to describe your energy/attention.

Day	Breakfast	Midmorning Snack	Energy/ Attention
Monday			
Tuesday			
Wednesday			
Thursday			
Friday			

What did you notice about your current eating patterns in relation to your energy level and attention span?

_____

_____

_____

_____

What changes, if any, will you make to maintain positive energy and attention levels?

_____

_____

_____

So what else do you need to do in the classroom?

_____

_____

_____

Learning Requires Tools: You Must Bring Them with You

Does a painter go to his job without his paintbrush?

Along with bringing the best you you can bring to the classroom, going to class also requires some prior planning. Bringing only you to class is usually not enough. Depending on the different and specific class requirements, you will need to bring different things with you. For most high school classes, the material requirements are fairly basic, but they are very necessary and include items such as writing utensils, paper, notebook, textbooks, and general things such as these. By the time you head to high school, needing to bring these items to class with you shouldn't even need to be mentioned—it should be understood. Heading to class without the basics is like leaving the house without your shoes; you just don't do it. Arriving to class unprepared takes your focus away from learning and getting the most out of class and creates distraction and anxiety.

Other classes may require additional items, and these items may require a special purchase or trip to the store. These may include calculators, math tools (compass, protractor), art supplies, a foreign language dictionary, etc. Although they go beyond the basics, if your teacher says they are necessary, then you need to obtain them promptly. Sometimes it is necessary to purchase textbooks, workbooks, or literature books. I have known many students who put off the purchase of these materials and then fall perilously behind in the assignments. Heading into October without the necessary materials will hinder your participation and learning, and probably your grades. If you are having trouble obtaining the necessary materials, inform your teacher as soon as possible for suggestions and assistance. Books and calculators can be very costly; perhaps your teacher has some ideas.

As different classes may require different tools, how do you intend to make sure you're prepared for each and every class, each and every day? This is done by planning and thinking. If you always bring what you need to class, then you're all set. If you find yourself frequently, or even occasionally, unprepared, keep in mind Key Element 2—Intend to Succeed, and Plan to Do Well—and try the following.

How to Avoid Showing up Unprepared

1. As you go through the day, give yourself the gift of time. *Pause* and ask yourself specific questions like: What classes do I have today? What will I need to bring for that class?

2. *Pause* in the morning as you're packing up your backpack to mentally walk yourself through your day at school. Think about that day's specific schedule, and ask yourself what you will need for that class. Then make sure you have it.

3. *Pause* at your locker. If you're using a locker in school, a similar procedure can be done before and between classes during the school day. Give yourself an extra minute at your locker to ask yourself, "What do I need for this next class?" This can save you not only time later but also a fair amount of stress.

4. *Pause* before leaving school for the day. Once again, walk yourself through each of your classes, making sure you are bringing home all you will need. This is also a good time to consult your agenda to see what you have for homework and be sure you are not leaving anything important at school.

5. *Pausing* at critical times of the day—before leaving the house, before leaving your locker, before leaving school—and mentally walking through where you are going and what you will need is a very useful skill that can be developed and become habit-forming.

6. Utilize visual cues. You might also post a list of what you need to bring on the inside of your locker door or somewhere at home where you are sure to see it. One student who frequently left something behind posted the following paper on his kitchen door, where he would be sure to see it every day before he left for school.

Stop
Do you have what you need?

Binder _____

Agenda _____

All textbooks _____

Backpack _____

And ...

All Homework _____

The day is yours!
Be all that you can be.

Make sure you bring everything you need to bring to the classroom with you.

What do you need for every class?

_____

_____

_____

_____

How will you remember the things that you need?

_____

_____

_____

Learning Is Interactive

Who is responsible for your learning in the classroom?

_____

_____

_____

_____

What is your role?

_____

_____

_____

_____

What is your teacher's role?

_____

_____

_____

_____

Learning requires the effort of two parties—the teacher and the student. As the teacher is conducting the class, you must be sure to be in charge of your actual learning. It's like that old adage, "You can lead a horse to water, but you cannot make it drink." Your teacher has prepared the lesson and delivers the lesson to you; you must take it from there.

You as a student have the ability to influence the quality of teacher instruction. Just as learning is interactive, teaching is also interactive. Your teacher will teach better to interested and involved students. Students who are actively listening and engaged will motivate and energize their teachers. The opposite is also true. Students who are not listening, are uninvolved, or cause distractions and disruptions will negatively impact a teacher's ability to teach as he/she has to spend more time on classroom management and less time actively teaching. Teachers choose to teach what they are teaching because they are passionate about the content area. Your involvement, or lack of involvement, will influence the quality of the instruction you receive. So, how do you remain interactive in class?

Learning Is Not a Spectator Sport

It's not enough just to show up to class and sit quietly. Have you ever gone to class and missed a huge amount of what the teacher is saying because you were having difficulty paying attention? This is bound to happen sometimes, and it happens to most people. Controlling how often and for how long it happens is something you can prepare for. Maintaining attention in the classroom requires a two-pronged approach, involving both the mind and the body. Let's address the mind first.

First—intend to learn. The first thing you can do actually occurs before you enter the classroom, and it involves having the right mind-set. That's right. As simple as it sounds, it is the first step. *Intend* to learn. *Intend* to pay attention. Remember, success doesn't just happen. It is intentional, and you must work for it.

As you enter your classroom, get your inner voice working. Keep in mind Key Element 1—Assign Value to What You Are Doing by seeing the importance of what you are learning.

Intend to leave the classroom with more than you entered with. Ask yourself questions like the following:

How might I use this?

How can this enrich me?

How might this make me a stronger, better prepared person for the world?

Second—give yourself a task. The purpose of giving yourself a task is that it will help you focus on the lesson at hand. Often you are already taking notes in class, but by giving yourself a specific task, you will enhance your interaction. Examples might be:

- o identify the big ideas of the presentation

- o raise questions about the content

- o think of three things you specifically want to remember

- o make a connection to something you already know

- o find something you want to relay to your family this evening at the dinner table

Third—get involved in class. By keeping yourself actively involved in the class, you keep yourself attentive and available to learn. If you find yourself drifting off, actively participate in some manner. Keep in mind Key Element 4 and the value of practice, as you practice the following methods of class participation.

Raise your hand and participate. This can be hard. You may feel self-conscious or feel you don't understand the material enough to participate. Participating in the classroom is like getting on the field during a game versus sitting on the bench. It might be intimidating at the beginning, but the more you do it, the more comfortable you will feel. So let's look at some baby steps for jumping into the participation game.

Answer questions in class. Some questions that the teachers ask are easier to answer than others; there may not even be a right or wrong answer. For instance, "How was your weekend? What did you do over the vacation? How did you feel when the main character in the story was incarcerated?" In some cases, you might even want to practice ahead of time for your participation debut. Especially in foreign language class, this can be helpful.

Ask questions when something is unclear to you or if you need something repeated. Asking a question in class is not only helpful to you; it is also helpful to your teacher as he/she assesses your level of understanding.

Choose a seat where you are noticeable to the teacher. When you do this, it will be more uncomfortable for you to lapse into a daydream state and tune out what is going on in the classroom.

Make eye contact with your teacher, pick up your pen or pencil, assume the ready-to-lear position, and you're on your way!

> You are what you repeatedly do.
> Excellence then, is not an act,
> but a habit.
>
> —Will Durant

Now, help your body pay attention.

To do this, be aware of what your body is doing. Practice what is called ***Whole Body Listening*** (Truesdale, 1990). This means getting your entire body into the game of learning. Here are some things you can do to assume the ready-to-learn position:

✓ Sit up tall.

✓ Face your body toward the teacher.

✓ Plant your feet squarely on the floor in front of you.

✓ Have your eyes and ears engaged on the teacher.

✓ Have your pencil or pen in hand.

Simply readjusting your body periodically sends you a reminder to stay focused and on task. Taking some deep breaths will bring an added boost of oxygen to your brain.

Other things you can do if you feel yourself getting restless as you sit in class is to unobtrusively stretch your muscles with leg, foot, neck, and straightening spine stretches. If you are working independently, or if you can do so without it causing a problem, stand up. Standing is a great way to wake your body up. If you're permitted to bring water into your classroom, take a sip of water. The bottom line is hold yourself accountable. Be mindful of paying attention, and have strategies that will help you. Think of some of your own ways to help yourself be more attentive in the classroom.

1. _____

2. _____

3. _____

Identify and Avoid Distractions

Friends or Foe?

School is a highly social setting. The mere fact that it is grouping large numbers of people of the same age together guarantees that social forces will be at work. School is also a place to practice and develop the social skills that are necessary now and in the future. Socializing is undeniably an important and essential part of the school experience. The problem arises when these social forces interfere with or usurp the other goals of attending school.

Your school day can essentially be divided into two parts: time inside the classroom and time outside of the classroom, meaning before and after school, in between classes, break time, lunchtime, and any other less structured times built into your school day.

Take a moment to identify the times in your day where you can interact with your friends.

_____

_____

_____

_____

Now take a moment to picture your classroom time and ask yourself, what is your time in the classroom really about?

_____

_____

_____

_____

I have always said to my students, "I'm pretty sure you will find another time to chat with your friends, but I'm less sure you'll find another time to learn what we are learning in class right now."

You're going to class every day, you might as well have something to show for it. This is your time to learn—you've paid for it with your time, and you deserve it. Being of the mind-set that you want to learn what is being presented to you, you want to take something away from these lessons, you want to enrich yourself and make yourself better prepared for your future, will go a long way in helping you succeed. Recognizing that your time in the classroom is really about these things is the first step.

Keep your personal goals, hopes, and dreams for your future close at hand, and remember that what you do each and every day matters.

So what about those friends? In the classroom, are they really friends or are they foes?

The ideal situation is to have a group of friends who are like-minded in their commitment to getting the most out of the educational experience as well as each and every class—friends who value their time spent in school and are focused on their futures. Both of my sons were fortunate to be in groups that wanted to succeed academically and had their sights set on attending competitive colleges. They were with friends who motivated each other to do well. But many students have not yet drawn the connections between what they do today and what they will be doing in a few short years.

So how do you handle your friends when they don't share your feelings on the importance of school? How do you handle your friends or other students when they are distracting you in class?

A student who is not actively and consistently involved in his or her educational experience can demonstrate this in several ways; some of these ways will have a greater impact on you than others. For our purposes, I am presenting three scenarios.

1. The chatty friend

2. The uninvolved, bored student

3. The disruptive student

All three of these can have a major impact on your own attitude and classroom experience, and need to be prepared for and guarded against.

Scenario 1—The Chatty Friend

You end up sitting next to a really good friend of yours in English class. You're trying to concentrate on the class discussion that is taking place on the setting of a novel and how this setting helped lead the characters to make the decisions they made. Meanwhile, your friend is trying to talk to you every time he or she thinks the teacher may be looking elsewhere. You know from previous experience that you have missed some key points because you were focusing on your friend and not the class. These points managed to find their way into tests you took, and of course, you didn't know them. You really don't want this to happen again. So how will you handle this?

Some suggestions my students have made include the following:

1.   Try talking to your friend honestly. Tell him or her that you're concerned about your grade, you'd like to do well, and that school is important to you.

2.   When your friend begins talking to you, you can:

   a.   Shift your position so that you're not quite as accessible to his or her comments.

   b.   Stay totally focused on the teacher or current speaker.

   c.   Quickly whisper, "Let's talk later. I want to hear this."

3.   Choose your seat wisely and away from your talkative friend.

Scenario 2—The Uninvolved, Bored Student

Here you might be thinking, *So what does that have to do with me? What can I do about uninvolved, bored students in my classroom?* This situation is actually a two-way street. Your attitude and actions as a student will either add or detract from the educational environment in your classroom, as will everyone else's.

An uninvolved, bored student adds nothing to the classroom environment. In fact, it is possible that his or her attitude will actually influence other students into acting in a similar manner. Behavior such as not participating, not contributing, and not raising your hand can spread throughout the classroom. Students may even begin to feel self-conscious if they display enthusiasm for the class. I'm sure you can picture this happening. So what can you do? First of all, be on guard against it. Be aware of someone else's attitude impacting the class and you in a negative manner. Second, keep doing what you're doing. Keep on raising your hand, asking questions, and staying involved. You also have the ability to influence what happens in your classroom. Be the change you want to see in the world!

Scenario 3—The Disruptive Student

Schools are essentially providing the public a service, and the public is paying for this service through their tax dollars. Or in the case of private schools, parents and students are paying the schools directly for these services. As in any other service that you pay for, you expect something in return. Disruptive students interfere with you getting what you expect and what you have paid for. Or if you are the disruptive student, then you are interfering with what other students have paid for. Rarely do students think of it this way.

So what can be done with students who are disruptive in class? First of all, it is a classroom management issue, and ultimately, it is the responsibility of the classroom teacher. That being said, there are things that students can do to discourage disruptions from fellow students. Ignoring disruptive behavior in the form of not laughing at remarks designed to get attention, or not looking at the individual, can be like not feeding a fire. You can also help lead by example and be attentive and hardworking in class. But since you are only one person, and there's no guarantee how the rest of the class will act, there is the possibility that these approaches won't solve the problem.

Hopefully while you are doing your part, your teacher is addressing this issue and you are seeing improvement. Just as you strategize and problem-solve your way through your schoolwork, your teachers will be strategizing and problem-solving their way through a classroom management situation. Skilled, experienced teachers typically have fewer problems in this area and often make adjustments and corrections so quickly you hardly realize there is a problem.

However, some problems and situations may not be adequately addressed. If you feel your education is being hampered because of another student, that what your teacher has or has not been doing isn't working for you, try talking to your teacher privately. He or she may have you change your seat or take other actions. You are entitled to an education, and measures should be taken to rein in students who prevent you from learning what you need to learn to move on to the next course.

Activity

1.   Think about disruptive students you have shared classes with. What were some of the things they did that interfered with the teacher teaching the class, with the students learning, and with the overall success of the classroom? How did you feel about it?

_____

_____

_____

_____

_____

2.   Think of "model" students you have shared classes with. How did they act in class? What were some of the specific things you noticed that they did? How did they add to the overall success of the classroom experience?

_____

_____

_____

_____

_____

Using the Computer: Yea or Nay

Many schools are adopting a BYOD (bring your own device) to class policy. Often, the policy states that individual teachers can decide if, when, and how electronic devices will be used. Many classrooms, and certainly even more at the college level, leave it up to the students to decide the answers to those questions. In fact, the trend is heading toward few, if any, restrictions on the use of electronic devices in classrooms, as they are becoming so integrated into today's culture.

It is clear that electronic devices are valuable and beneficial; certainly all of us can list numerous ways this is so. But what are the detriments and limitations to electronic devices in the classroom and at home for school use?

What do you see as the positives to computer use in the classroom?

Positives:

_____

_____

_____

_____

What do you see as the negatives to computer use in the classroom?

Negatives:

_____

_____

_____

_____

The important question is: how are *you,* or how will you, be using your electronic device? Is it to the benefit or detriment of your educational experience?

This is a question that is being asked more and more in regard to student learning. Recently, numerous studies have been conducted regarding student learning and electronic devises. One subject of these studies looks at how students take notes in the classroom—whether it's by computer or by hand.

You may initially think that taking notes on your computer during class lectures is more effective because you are able to type faster than you can handwrite and therefore get more of what your teacher is saying down in your notes. Studies are yielding surprising results and have found that many students who took handwritten notes performed better on quizzes and tests than their counterparts taking notes using an electronic device. The reason for this discrepancy is twofold. Students who were writing by hand could not possibly record every word their teacher said. Therefore, they were inclined to better process the information, filtering out the main ideas and what was important, thus giving them more interaction with the material as it was being presented and a greater understanding. Second, it has been found that the actual act of handwriting utilizes portions of the brain that are connected to memory, thus increasing the likelihood that students will remember what has been taught.

Electronics and Unintended Consequences

Students who utilize electronic devices in the classroom and at home need to exercise a form of self-discipline and self-monitoring that is not required in the same way as when working without an electronic device. The temptation to stray from the task at hand and to check e-mail, search other sites, and connect with friends proves too hard to resist for many. The very nature of the electronic device makes it difficult for the teacher/professor/parent to see exactly what the student is working on. With the screen up at an angle that blocks views, or a darkened screen that doesn't allow someone else to see what is being worked on, a student can be checking social media, playing a game, chatting with another student, or simply researching something else entirely. Often the student's facial expression, of rapt interest or mounting enthusiasm, can be a dead giveaway that they are not writing about the causes of the Cold War. Students often think, *Oh, I'll just check this for a moment*, and the continuity of learning is broken or abandoned all together.

This frequent shifting of attention from learning to other things is proving to negatively impact learning in ways that were not previously known. Recent studies show that attending to multiple things at one time, or multitasking, is resulting in a significant drop in productivity and quality of work. The brain is not geared to multitask and focus on multiple things at once. Valuable ground and time is lost as the brain transitions from one area of focus to another.

The successful use of electronic devices in the classroom and at home requires a certain degree of maturity and self-discipline that often is not present. Sometimes the best solution is simply to put electronic devices away unless they are specifically necessary for an assignment.

In addition, the very act of having a screen between the student and the teacher can create a barrier that is effective for hiding behind. You look busy, but you're really not. You look like you're on track, but are you? There also is now, quite literally, a wall between the teacher and student.

Ultimately, in today's world, the responsibility is yours. Electronic devices are vital, and they provide proven value, but if you are one of those who find themselves frequently straying from the topic at hand, you must think of ways to monitor yourself. At school, that might even mean abandoning the use of an electronic device in certain classes. When at home, that might mean building in specific breaks to check your social media and holding yourself accountable for not doing so during the work periods—for example, forty minutes of work with all electronic devices out of reach and out of sight, followed by ten minutes to check messages, email, etc. My personal recommendation is to *unplug* as much as possible and allow your brain to do the uninterrupted work of learning.

Electronic Books versus Printed Books

Which is better for students: an e-book or printed book? This is an ongoing debate, with many schools offering both and leaving it up to personal preference. The three largest publishing companies that cater to the k–12 educational market offer numerous options for both, and both are surprisingly costly. Determining factors in making this decision include:

- Accessibility—how reliable is Wi-Fi, both at home and at school?

- Is the weight of textbooks an issue?

- Is the use of a tablet or electronic device going to be distracting for the student, or will it be engaging and keep him or her involved?

- Does the student like to highlight and annotate the text when reading?

- And finally, how successful are you with the system you are using? If using an e-book just opens the door to a variety of excuses (my tablet broke, the internet was down, etc.), then it's not working.

- Find out what works most successfully for you, and know that what works may be different at different times and in different situations.

5

The Homework Piece

Homework is a reality in high school. For many students, homework can become a source of dread and stress, but the majority of students will take homework in stride, viewing it as part and parcel of the high school experience. Often homework makes up a significant portion of a course grade and contributes to test readiness, so it is in your best interest to work out a successful plan for addressing homework. It is important to make sure your homework is completed well, is done in a timely fashion, is not overly stressful, and enhances your grade.

As in everything else you do that is school related, the first task is *to assign a value* to what you are doing.

Why is this task important for you, and how can it help you? Homework assignments may serve a variety of valuable purposes:

1. **Homework is an opportunity *to practice* and reinforce skills taught in the classroom.**

It is the added reinforcement gained by practicing a skill again and again that will make it automatic and better cement it to memory. Good examples of the benefits of practicing involve solving math problems and the memorization of foreign language vocabulary.

2. **Homework may be assigned *to prepare* you for an upcoming lesson.**

It may be necessary for building background knowledge prior to the lesson. This also includes assigned readings in fiction and nonfiction texts that there is just not time to read during class but that will be studied and discussed.

3. **Homework may be assigned *to develop* deeper thought and creativity.**

This may be done through assigned writings, reports, or projects.

4.   Homework helps *to build* specific and valuable lifelong skills.

By successfully managing your homework, you are practicing and mastering invaluable skills that will be required of you in the future: time management, task initiation, task commitment, and organizational skills.

Homework Survey

Respond to the following statements with: Yes, No, NI—Needs Improvement

I see the value in doing my homework.	
I have a specific place where I study and do my homework.	
My study area is free of distractions.	
My study area contains the materials I need to do my work.	
My work place is well organized and free of distracting clutter.	
My work place is comfortable for me and encourages work.	
I know when I will be doing my homework each day.	
I have the books and resources I need when I sit down to work.	
I have written my assignments in a planner of some sort.	
I pack up my books and work when I am done.	
I tidy and restock my work area when I am done.	

How Have You Managed Homework So Far?

What are some of the tools and strategies you have in place to make homework a *successful* part of your school picture?

1. _____

_____

_____

_____

2. _____

_____

_____

_____

3. _____

_____

_____

_____

What are some of the challenges you have had regarding homework?

1. _____

_____

_____

_____

2. _____

_____

_____

_____

3. _____

_____

_____

_____

The Study Environment

Establishing a study environment that is conducive for work and concentration, and also serves to motivate you, will go a long way in helping you achieve homework success.

What makes a good study environment?

1. _____

2. _____

3. _____

4. _____

By simply answering that question, you are already putting thought into where and how you will study.

Below are some suggestions for setting up your study environment.

1. Choose your location carefully.

Having a place that is specifically designated for studying and related schoolwork will create an environment conducive for working. A regular location in which to work sends an automatic mental cue that says, "This is the place where I work." When you put aside a specific location and spend time setting it up, you create an environment that is on your side and that automatically gets you into a working mind-set.

Sitting on the couch in the family room, with the TV on and your siblings playing, may be fine if you're collating papers or coloring in a map, but it is far from optimum if you are writing a paper or studying for your precalculus test. Divided attention will result in dividing your grade. Shifting attention from one task to another has been found to be detrimental to concentration, learning, and the production of quality work.

By the same token, lying on your bed while doing your work may make you just a little too relaxed. It is also not the most effective way to take notes, juggle textbooks and papers, and do challenging math problems. But the bottom line is this: the proof is in the pudding. Is your work done? Is it done well? How are your grades?

2. Keep it distraction free.

A tenth grader once asked me how I felt about students doing their homework in their bedrooms. Before I answered, I asked him why he asked me this. He responded that his mom had started making him do his work at the kitchen table while she prepared dinner or otherwise putters around. My guess is that after years of his heading up to his room to do his work and never actually getting it done, his mother had had enough.

You may be thinking at this point, *This is high school! Who needs their mother to monitor their schoolwork?* Certainly by high school, the hope is that students can work independently and stay on task, but over the past decade, specific distractions have increased that make it harder to obtain a limited-distraction environment.

Technology is a major villain here. Cell phones, computers with social media sites, and the television make it hard to work for any period of time without being lured away. Think ahead how you will manage these distractions so that at the end of a three-hour study session in your room, you have three hours of work to show for it.

The more time you spend distracted and off task, the longer your homework will take you. Shifting your attention from the task at hand to your phone so that you can check your messages or send a text disrupts your concentration and leads to poor homework performance.

3. Make sure it meets basic requirements.

The location you choose should be set up specifically for your work. Does it have the basic physical things you need?

    a. Tabletop or desk top

    b. Good chair

    c. Adequate working space for books and a computer

    d. Lighting

    e. Storage space for necessary materials

4. Has necessary supplies.

Once your study environment has been selected, it is important to set it up with all the materials you will need. Valuable time is often wasted looking for basic things like pencils, calculators, rulers, etc. Not having what you need can serve as a convenient excuse for not getting your work done or for not completing it. Set up your workstation ahead of time with all the supplies you envision yourself needing.

Below, make a list of the items your study station should have:

1. _____

2. _____

3. _____

4. _____

5. _____

Now that you have these things, it is important that you replenish these supplies as needed. It's not that you set yourself up once and you are set for life. As things run low, be sure to replenish them, so that time will not be lost the next time you sit down to work.

5. Organize frequently

Organization, like anything else, is easier if you keep up with it. A neat, well-organized environment is one that invites you to work, not discourages you from a visit. Toward the end of each study session, spend a minute or two putting things back in order. This serves many purposes.

- It will be easier to get started when you return.

- It will be easier to find everything you need when you are working.

- It decreases the likelihood that you will leave anything behind that you might need the next day for school. In tidying up, you are more likely to see the book you need tomorrow, or see that you hadn't packed up your homework yet.

6. Alternate Locations

In some situations, you may not have a work area that is exclusively yours. Perhaps you work on the dining room table, or in a parent's office, or somewhere else that is a shared space. Perhaps you are not able to leave your supplies there in between your study sessions. In that case, I recommend what I refer to as a portable workstation. This may be a container, tote, file box, or something else that you can take with you. Inside of this, keep all the things you would normally have at your workstation.

You may also choose, or the situation may dictate, that you work elsewhere. A prime example of this may be your school library. Often students find they have time between the end of the school day and a sporting event or other school function. This time can be well spent on homework and study, and the school library provides a good location for this purpose. A local town library may also provide a more secluded and motivating work space. When I was in college and struggling with my chemistry course, I chose a spot in our school library on the third floor, where no one would find me and I could immerse myself in my studies without any interruptions.

Activity

1. Set up your work area at home.

2. What makes this a good work area?

    _____

    _____

3. Place a picture of your work area here.

Plan Your Work and Work Your Plan
(Your Homework, That Is!)

So, now your study environment is all set up and it's time to get to work. How can you help yourself be most productive, while also being sure that no matter what your workload, you are prepared for tomorrow?

Plan Your Work and Work Your Plan

This can actually start as you are leaving the school building, or walking or driving home from school.

When my sons were in middle school, we would drive to and from school together, as I taught in the same school they attended. On our ride home, I would generally ask, "How does the homework look for tonight?" They would then walk through their classes, thinking briefly about what they needed to do and estimating roughly how much time they would need for each subject. If they had a sports practice or a game that night, they'd have to ask themselves when they would put in the necessary time. Perhaps they would need to divide their work time into a session before the practice and a session afterward. If the evening was open, it was a great time to get ahead on things, especially if another night was going to be busy.

Think about what you need to do and approximately how much time you will need to do it.

This is the preliminary step in successfully addressing your homework responsibilities. As you mentally walk through your homework load and visit each and every subject that you have, ask yourself: what exactly needs to be done, and about how long will be needed for each assignment? Soon you will have an estimation of how long in total you will need. Be sure to refer to your agenda so you don't overlook anything. I recommend that my students number the items in their agenda according to priority and then in parentheses put approximately how much time they think they will need to spend on each task.

Try doing that now.

1. Mentally walk through your homework load, visiting each and every class.

2. List what needs to be done in each class, and approximately how long you think it will take you.

3.   How much time will you need in all?

_____

4.   Number the items in the order you will do them (prioritize your work).

_____

_____

Determine when you are most productive.

When will you do your work? As you observe yourself at work, you may start to notice that you are more productive at certain times of the day versus others. Some students like to complete as much work as possible prior to dinner, while others may need a break after school before settling down. Pay close attention to what seems to be better for you, and try to work with that, knowing that sometimes, it may not matter what is "best" for you; it just has to be done anyway. Remember that energy levels wax and wane, and you are bound to experience fatigue as the evening wears on. Suggestions here include:

-   Schedule work that requires greater concentration for earlier in the study session, and work that will be mentally less challenging for later on.

-   Break up your challenging workload with intermittent assignments that are less challenging.

-   Change up the way you study. Try standing up. Use markers and a white board. Change rooms or locations for a specific assignment.

When do you think you work best?

Be sure to start early enough.

This is where estimating how long you need to complete your homework is helpful. If you've estimated that you will need about two hours, and you're exhausted and done for the day by 9:30, you certainly wouldn't begin at 8:30.

Use your agenda (at school and at home)

As you sit down to plan and begin your work, don't just count on memory. Take out your agenda and confirm what needs to be done. This will help you set up your study plan for the evening. As you complete your assignments, check them off in your agenda. Marking work as completed leads to a sense of accomplishment and encouragement.

On nights that you find yourself quite busy, or facing more than you think you can complete, it is important to prioritize your workload.

Prioritize Your Assignments

High priority—must be done today.

Secondary—should be started today if it is to be done well, but there is still time.

On the radar—it's coming up. If you have time left over, or a light night of homework, it is never too early to begin working on a long-term assignment. Ideally, you begin right away, working on these assignments bit by bit. For students with a particularly busy schedule, long-term assignments might best be addressed during weekend days, especially if a large portion of a weekend day can be set aside to work on these. When done this way, it eases the load and stress during the weekdays when there is always other work to do.

Studying for tests and quizzes should also be built into your plans and can be addressed with this priority system. However, it is always best to study over a period of a few days vs. all at once the night before.

For those of you who want or require a more concrete form of planning your work, you may find that setting up a work/study schedule each evening before you begin is helpful. You might casually jot down a schedule for yourself, like the one below. Instead of saying, I'm going to sit down from 4:00 to 6:00 to work, you might break it down as follows:

Sample Study Schedule

4:00–4:45—First draft of compare/contrast assignment

4:45–5:15—Spanish vocab

5:15–5:25—Break

5:25–6:00—Math

Note to self—If I complete everything early, take a look at science requirement sheet for new project.

You may prefer something more structured. There are many templates available for managing your time and work. A good idea is to print out several at a time so they are ready to use. They can be as simple as the ones provided here that many of my students use.

Daily Schedule

Time	Subject/Activity
3:00	
4:00	
5:00	
6:00	
7:00	
8:00	
9:00	
10:00	

You may choose to use a sequence chart, simply outlining the order in which you will approach your tasks.

Sample Evening Sequence Chart

First: Unpack and set up work area
Next: Do vocab workbook
Next: Read *Catcher in the Rye*
Next: Algebra—page 67, 1–19 odds
Next: ?
Next: ?
Last: Pack up all work and materials for tomorrow

Fill in your own Evening Sequence Chart

First: Unpack and set up work area
Next:
Next:
Next:
Next:
Next:
Last: Pack up all work and materials for tomorrow

Does Your Book Bag Come Home Every Night but Remain Unopened?

If you repeatedly tell yourself that you have no work to do, and your backpack or book bag remains on the floor, unopened until you leave for school the next day, try this:

1. Open your backpack or book bag

2. Begin organizing and going through your binders and textbooks.

3. Identify one thing to work on and do it!

4. Put it back where it belongs.

Sometimes the simple act of opening your bag and rummaging through your books and binders can be enough to spur you on.

Homework Troubleshooting

You may have the best intentions for doing all your work but find that it is hard to stay on task. Even though you have been sitting at your desk for quite a while, very little work has actually been done.

While you may have difficulty staying on task, your work will still be due. Utilize strategies to help you succeed.

Intend to Learn (Remember the things we have talked about so far.)

1. Assign value to what you are doing. See the importance of the particular assignment you are working on.

2. Remember The Three Big Reasons to Do Well. You get to take everything you learn with you. Doing well increases your options in life. You're practicing the skills you need to be successful.

3. Be your own cheerleader. Get the little voice in your head working for you, telling you things like: I'm going to get the most out of this work that I can. I'm going to come away knowing more than I did when I sat down. This is going to be my best work yet.

Set goals

Sometimes setting mini-goals along the way can help keep you on track. Because you see a beginning and a clear end, it may be easier to stay with it. Setting goals like "I'm going to complete problems 1 through 10 before I take my break" can be helpful.

Exclude distractions/*unplug*

So much time is lost with interruptions and distractions. In order to be most effective, eliminate distractions from your workspace. Common distractions include the phone, social media, and other sites on the computer. You might think you can concentrate on your school work while periodically checking your phone, texting someone back, or checking social media sites, but the truth is, your brain can only focus effectively on one thing at a time. Every time you pull your attention away from the task at hand, even momentarily, you lose time, concentration, and progress.

Many students turn their phones off during their work sessions, turning them on during breaks, or at the conclusion of their work, almost as a reward. Completely turning off your phone or computer if you are not using it for your work can be a hard thing to force yourself to do, but it is the *best* thing you can do to help yourself stay on track.

Use a timer

A timer can be a versatile and effective tool.

Using a timer helps with task initiation.

For students who tend to procrastinate, it can be used to signal the beginning of a session. For example, try setting the timer fifteen minutes before you plan to begin your work. This way you're priming yourself, much like the parent who gives their child a five-minute warning, alerting them to the fact that in five minutes they will be leaving the park, ending play time, or whatever it may be. This gives the child transition time—time to mentally and emotionally prepare for what will be next. Setting the timer fifteen minutes or so before you plan to work can serve a similar purpose. "I can do what I want for the next fifteen minutes—I can get everything I think I'll need organized, etc." and then when the timer goes off, it's time to begin.

Using a timer assists with focus during the task.

A problem students have often shared is maintaining attention while working. Setting a timer establishes a beginning and end time so work doesn't appear endless. I don't recommend setting the timer for two hours if you are someone who tends to wander off track. Depending on your concentration level and/or the subject at hand, you might set the timer for as little as twenty or thirty minutes. As you gradually increase your ability to concentrate, you can increase the time that you set your timer, but insist on staying completely on task for that amount of time.

Establish at the beginning exactly what you plan on completing in that period of time. When the buzzer has gone off and you have completed that task, you have completed something and feel successful. You will find that you are more on task and more productive during that specific time allotment than you may have been previously for a greater period of time. If there is more work, after a short break, repeat the process, again establishing at the beginning what you hope to achieve during that thirty-minute time span.

Setting the timer, and knowing that you will focus exclusively for just that amount of time, often yields terrific results. If you find your mind wandering from the task to other things you'd like to do—like message a friend, get a snack, make a call, etc.—simply jot that thought down on a piece of paper, and continue with the work you are doing. This sends a message to your brain that you will attend to that task, but at another time.

Vary your routine within the study block

After you have prioritized your workload, how you go about completing that work is a matter of preference, and may vary day-to-day depending on specific assignments. However, if you find you have a considerable amount of work in one subject and find yourself drifting off and losing focus, a frequently used strategy is to put that work aside for a while and work on something else. It's similar to starting in on your roast beef and then switching to your potato for a while. You're not done with your roast beef; you're just attending to something else for a while.

Schedule and take a break

As you tire and notice your concentration waning, it is a good idea to take a short break. A movement break is a good idea, as is a drink or snack break if you feel your energy waning. But put a limit on your break time before you take it so that it doesn't stretch into time that you really don't have. In fact, this is another good opportunity to use your timer.

Summarize and hold yourself accountable as you go along

So how do you know if you've stayed on task? How do you really know if your time reading and studying has been productive or not? Don't wait until the end of the session to see if it's been a success.

Just because you are sitting at your desk and "working" doesn't necessarily guarantee you are getting something out of your time. Pause frequently as you are reading or studying to restate the information and summarize the main points. Imagine you are explaining the content to someone else. If you are unable to talk about what you have read or studied, that is a good indication that you have not absorbed much of the content.

If you are reading a passage in a text, try the RCRC (read, cover, recite, check) technique (Archer and Gleason, 1989) or something similar. This is as it sounds; read a paragraph or selection, cover it up, see if you can recite back to yourself the main points, and check to see if you recited what was important. If you are studying for a quiz or test, try testing yourself to see exactly what you have taken away from the lesson.

Specific methods for holding yourself accountable during reading assignments and while studying for tests and quizzes can be found in both the Studying and Reading sections of this book.

Avoiding the, "Oops! I left that at home!"

After you've put effort into your homework and you're feeling pleased with yourself and ready for class the next day, nothing feels worse than leaving your work at home. Not only can it throw you off and put you in an instant bad mood, it can also lower your grade—and you did the work! How do you prevent this from happening?

Forethought and organization are the keys to prevention.

As you complete your work and are ready to wrap up for the evening, there are a few things you can do that can to prevent the, "Oops, I left that at home," problem.

1. Pack your bag the night before.

Plan on packing your bag when you complete your work. This will not only prevent you from leaving work behind, but it also will help avoid the morning rush. The fewer details you have to attend to in the morning, the better off you are.

2. Scan your work area and room.

After you've packed your bag, scan your work area and room to be sure you are not leaving anything vital behind.

3. Tidy your work area.

Tidying your work area when you are done is an added precaution against leaving something important behind that may be hidden under a book or paper. It also serves the dual purpose of presenting a welcoming work environment the next day when you sit down to work again.

4. Post a reminder list on your door, if necessary.

If you are someone who tends to leave things behind, like your lunch, backpack, books, or homework, you might want to post something on the door you exit out of every day, like the "*Stop*, Do You Have What You Need" poster seen earlier in this book, or develop a little mantra as you double-check to see if you have everything before you leave: "books, homework, agenda, backpack, books, homework, agenda, backpack, books, homework, agenda, backpack." This is a final measure of insurance that you won't get to school unprepared and face a day of stress and misery.

Problems with Procrastination?

When it's time to get to work, does this sound like you?

-Uh … I don't have any work to do.

-I'm really not that good at it.

-I don't want to right now.

-Okay, right after I finish doing x, y, and z.

Procrastination often presents itself as poor time management, but it is more complex than that. Work and responsibilities often take a backseat to short-term, more instantly pleasurable rewards, such as video games, texting, emailing, snacking, hanging out with friends, or other optional activities. Students overemphasize the positive benefit of these other activities and underemphasize the positive feelings they will have tomorrow when everything is done. Often it is not until the night before something is due, when the deadline looms ahead like a cement wall to their speeding train, that they actually kick into action. The problem with this is that some students actually start to think they work better under the pressure that is created by having to work under extreme time constraints. This is not only dangerous (as something could certainly happen that could cause you not to complete the work), but it is also faulty thinking, as it's not that you perform better under stress, you just no longer have a choice. It also creates an enormous amount of avoidable stress. Unfortunately, every time a deadline is met after procrastinating, it reinforces this faulty belief that "you work better under pressure," when in reality the following are true:

1. You don't have the benefit of running your work by your teacher to be sure you are on the right track.

2. You have less time (perhaps no time) to really edit and proofread your work the way you would like to.

3. You have no time to redo things that you know you could have done better.

4. Something unexpected could come up, preventing you from doing your work that night.

In the case of procrastinating when studying for tests by cramming all the studying in the night or two before the exam, current research supports more study sessions distributed over more days, rather than larger chunks of study time over fewer or even one session. You're better off starting to study for Friday's test on Monday and studying every day of the week than you are studying only on Thursday, even if you spend the same amount of time in total. In addition, saving everything for the last day almost always ensures you will have little sleep that night. That can certainly work against you the next day, especially if you are testing.

It's not always as simple as wanting to do something else instead of your schoolwork. Students procrastinate for other reasons too.

~The work may seem too challenging, too overwhelming, or just too long.

~Students might fear that whatever they do won't be good enough.

~Students might procrastinate because they are "not really in the mood" or "too tired to start" and convince themselves that if they are not "in the mood" or "too tired," the end product won't be that good. I equate that to a runner going out for their daily run. They may not always be in the mood to run, or might feel a little tired that day, but once they get started, they get more and more into the swing of it, and it gets easier.

Procrastinators with these excuses mistakenly think that tomorrow things will be different. In this case, I use the following riddle: What's always coming, but never comes? Tomorrow. Sure, tomorrow will be different. You'll be one step closer to your deadline, or perhaps you will have passed your deadline, and that is the only thing that will be different.

Regardless of the reasons for procrastination, there are things you can do to address this issue.

1. **Recognize** that you are delaying a task. If you notice that you are actually looking for other things to do (text friends, check social media, have a snack, watch a show, do a chore around the house, etc.) rather than the task at hand, you are procrastinating.

2. **Reflect** on why you are delaying the specific task, and be honest with yourself.

   a. Do I tell myself I have lots of time? If so, how has *that* worked out in the past?

   b. Am I not really clear on what I need to do? If that's the case, then the sooner I find out, the better. Is there some part of it I can get started on anyway?

   c. Does it seem like it will take a long time so I'm waiting for a day when I have a lot of time? All you will have tomorrow is less time left before it is due. What portion of it can you start or complete today?

   d. Am I telling myself tomorrow will be a better day to do it? Really? Tomorrow will most likely be worse because of added pressure and guilt caused by not getting started.

Recognizing that you are procrastinating, and thinking about some of the reasons why you might be doing so is an important first step. But there are also some actions you can take that may be helpful.

How do the following statements relate to procrastination or something else that you would like to change?

Doing more of the same gets you more of the same.

_____

_____

_____

_____

If you want something to change, you have to change what you are doing.

_____

_____

_____

_____

3. **Take Action**: You have recognized that you procrastinate, and you have reflected on the possible reasons you do so. Now it is time to change this habit that has worked against you. This ties into Key Element 2—Intend to Succeed, and Plan to Do Well. It is essential that you establish conditions that support your goals. This is done by adding controls to your environment and your time so they work for you rather than against you. Create conditions that are "on your side." Below are some strategies my students have implemented and have found helpful.

  a. Set up a work area. Is it free from distractions? Does it have all the necessary materials? Having a well-set-up work space sends a clear message to your brain that this is where you work. This is where you get things done. (See "The Study Environment" section.)

  b. As soon as you arrive home, bring your backpack/books directly to your work area. Immediately take out what you need to do, going so far as to open your books to the pages you need to work on and setting up any paper and supplies you might need. Example: open the math book to page 216, and put out a piece of paper, pencil, and calculator. This will make it a lot easier to actually sit down and begin your work when it is time. You are all set up and ready to go.

  c. Utilize a timer to signal it's time to get to work. This addresses the common issue of delaying the start of your daily work. (See "Homework Troubleshooting" section.)

  d. You can do anything for seven minutes. Often a task looms large and serves as a deterrent. Do something for seven minutes and see what happens.

  e. Accept no excuses. Even if you are not crystal clear on what it is you are supposed to do (something procrastinators will frequently convince themselves of), sit and work anyway. Begin. Find a small piece of the assignment that you _can_ do. Make a list of questions for your teacher. Often by getting started, you are able to figure things out. Hold yourself accountable, and work for the allotted time you planned to work.

f. Fill out a Problem-solving Strategy Worksheet

g. As always, remember the Four Key Elements of School Success:

   1. See the value in what you are doing.

   2. Intend to succeed at this task, and plan accordingly.

   3. Cheer yourself on with a focused and supportive inner voice.

   4. Remember, you are practicing important skills that you need now and will continue to need later in life. These skills include the ability to get started on a task and the ability to complete a task.

Long-Term Assignments

Many students with will openly declare that they have trouble with long-term assignments. Although they acknowledge this, they find it difficult to change their patterns of behavior. What is supposed to be an opportunity for in-depth learning, individual creativity, and the practicing of important lifelong skills instead becomes a game of beat the clock with increasing stress and anxiety, and a finished product that is less than it could have been. Long-term assignments are the procrastinator's nightmare. But the good news is that with every long-term assignment you are given, you get to practice and reinforce the positive skills of time management, task initiation, problem solving, and goal setting, among others.

Below are suggestions for managing long-term assignments:

1.   Use a separate pocket folder for all things pertaining to the assignment. This serves two purposes; 1) provides a consolidated place to keep the assignment directions, notes, articles you've printed out, etc., and 2) it makes it easier for you to start each work session as you know where everything is.

2.   Be sure you understand the assignment and seek clarification right away if needed. On the first day the assignment is given, thoroughly look over the directions, making a list of any questions you may have for your teacher. Too many students state they are "unclear" as to what they need to do when they first receive the assignment. The problem arises when they remain "unclear" week after week.

3.   Mark up the directions by highlighting, underlining, and circling key parts of the assignment so you are sure to complete all parts in the specified manner.

4.   Throughout the duration of the assignment, keep the directions and rubric, if you have been given one, handy to be sure you are staying on track and addressing all the important components of the assignment.

5.   Record the due date in your agenda or on the calendar you use, and count how many days you have to complete the task. Plan to finish at least one day early so you have time to thoroughly look things over and make any final changes.

6.   Break the assignment down into smaller, workable segments. Using your calendar, record when you plan on doing each task. Be sure to distribute the workload accordingly, always mindful of the deadline(s) your teacher has assigned.

7.   At the end of each work session, make a checklist of any new thoughts or questions you have, any notes to self or things you specifically want to accomplish the next time you sit down. Put that in the front of your pocket folder so you will see it when you begin working the next time.

8.   If you find yourself procrastinating when it's time to sit down the next time and stick to your scheduled plan, implement strategies from the "Procrastinating" section, including the seven-minute rule. You can do anything for seven minutes, and once you get going, you will build up momentum and be on your way.

6

Preparing for Tests and Quizzes

Okay, so you're looking like the model student in class; you're well fed, well rested, and well exercised. You're attentive, interactive, and always prepared with your assignments. Are you all set and firmly on the road to success? Not quite. You're certainly heading in the right direction, and success is within your sights, but there's another huge component to your educational experience: assessments.

Let's take a moment to look at your thoughts about and experiences with tests and quizzes.

What are your thoughts when you first hear you will be having a test?

_____

_____

_____

_____

How do you prepare for tests and quizzes?

_____

_____

_____

_____

How do you perform on tests and quizzes? Does it depend on the class?

_____

_____

_____

_____

Do your test and quiz grades usually help or hinder your overall grade?

_____

_____

_____

_____

Why Is Testing Important?

While you might think testing exists simply to create anxiety in students, when done right, testing serves some very important functions. Seeing the purpose and value of assessments is the first step in achieving success in the testing arena.

Informs the Teacher

First of all, assessments serve to inform the teacher. You may be looking at tests solely as a way for your teacher to determine what you know, but tests actually yield much more than that. By testing a student and a class, a teacher also receives feedback as to how well he or she conveyed the information he or she was teaching. Not only are teachers seeing if *you* were successful, but they are also seeing if *they* were successful. Were they going too fast? Is there a particular section they need to revisit with the class? Are there students who need additional support in a specific area? Remember, the goal is *education*, not getting a score. A test is feedback. It is a way to measure how things are going along the journey of education.

Allows Students to Pause and Process

Second, tests allow students to pause and process what they have learned up until that point. Students need time to review and reflect upon new information and ideas. They need time to formulate questions about what they have learned, and to monitor their understanding before adding additional information or leaving a topic behind. Pausing along the path of acquiring new information to prepare for a test provides the opportunity for students to think deeply about what they have learned and to incorporate their new knowledge with preexisting knowledge. The actual act of taking the test can also contribute to the learning process by affording students the opportunity to apply what they have learned and connect the dots of their learning.

Reinforces Memory

Last, testing assists in reinforcing memory. When preparing for an exam, students review and reflect upon what they have learned. In doing so, they are reinforcing the brain's memory connections, increasing the likelihood that what was learned will stay with them. Quizzing and testing is a form of retrieval practice, meaning you have learned the material and are able to retrieve it from your memory. Experiments conducted in foreign language instruction found that students who were repeatedly tested on information were more likely to commit that information to long-term memory than students who just studied the information. They determined it was the actual act of retrieving the information from memory versus simply reviewing already learned material that allowed them to recall the foreign language vocabulary for a longer period of time (Karpicke and Roediger, 2008). So if you want to remember something throughout the semester and for life, continually test yourself on it.

How Do You Best Prepare for Tests and Quizzes?

By *keeping up in the first place* and by *being a test-ready student.*

What does *that* mean?

How many students have said things like: "I studied for this, I really did, but I still did poorly." Or more specifically, "I studied for three hours last night, and I still didn't do well." Or, "I suffer from test anxiety, and that's why I do poorly."

Let me ask you a few questions.

Would you perform in a piano recital if you hadn't practiced?

Would you get in a plane with a pilot who never practiced landings?

Does your basketball, football, or lacrosse team only go to games and never practices?

What is the purpose of practice?

1. _____

2. _____

3. _____

If a sports team got together the day of a big game, out of shape and never having played together, would they be ready to face a team that has been training for weeks?

The answer is no. And just like athletes, musicians, and pilots, you have to practice. Only in this case, practice is in the form or preparing ahead of time for tests. And here's the thing—just like the examples above, you have to prepare all along the way, not just the night before. *Good test and quiz preparation actually begins the first day of class.*

Are you doing your work just to get it done? _____

Are you scrambling to make the deadline? _____

If the answer to either one or both of those questions is yes, then the actual learning of the material is taking a backseat. When students are scrambling, or doing work just to meet a deadline or get it out of the way, they are not primarily focusing on the learning of the material. By test time, this will catch up to you.

You must *learn* as you go, not just complete the work as you go. So much of high school work is cumulative, building on concepts and content that has gone before. You must be fully present in class and actively hold yourself accountable to what is being taught, or you run the risk of being irrevocably lost and left behind.

I suggest you give yourself a gift. Give yourself the gift of time. Start your daily work early enough so that you don't feel pressured, so you have the time to practice the good reading and learning techniques that will lead to a greater understanding of the material being presented. Hold yourself accountable for the learning as you go along, not just for completing the task.

It wasn't raining when Noah built the ark.
—Unknown

How does the quote above relate to preparing for tests and quizzes?

_____

_____

_____

_____

That's Right—You Have to Prepare Ahead of Time!

1. Prepare Ahead of Time

The first part of preparing for tests actually begins before a test is even announced. It begins the first day you step into class, and it is continuous. This is so important that I will repeat it. Preparing for a test begins the first day you step into a class, and it is continuous. The best way to learn what is being presented is by *keeping up in the first place,* by keeping up with all assignments and holding yourself accountable for understanding the material being taught each and every day.

If you snooze through a unit and think you're going to be able to catch up a night or two before the exam, eventually, if not immediately, your luck will run out. Content is best learned and absorbed by being reinforced over time. That is why when you simply cram for a test, just for the sake of taking the test the next day, it tends not to stay with you for the long term. This will definitely come back to haunt you during midterm and final exams when you are responsible for everything that has been taught all along the way.

Along with doing your work and paying attention in class, *see your teacher as soon as there is something you don't understand.* Be sure to learn as you go. Don't save it all until right before the test and then see your teacher. It will become clear to your teacher that you were uninvolved during the unit and are now scrambling to survive. While this is not a good way to make an impression, it is better than not seeing your teacher at all and failing.

Having a test or quiz should not come as a shock to you. As your school year progresses, you will be able to anticipate upcoming tests and quizzes even before they are announced.

Depending on the type of test or quiz, you will have varying amounts of time to prepare, but if you have been preparing ahead by being attentive in class, doing all assignments, and seeing your teachers along the way when you need assistance, *you will be as test ready as you can be.*

2. Have a Study Plan

The second part of preparing for a test or quiz occurs *immediately* after the test has been announced. Here are some suggestions I have made to my students.

   a. Get out the agenda!

   I encourage my students to write the test in *red* on the date the test will be given, and then plan their study time backward from that date. If the test is on Friday, write it in your agenda in red on Friday. Determine how many days of preparation you think you will need, and write that in also. If you need three days, you would write "study for test" on Tuesday, Wednesday, and Thursday.

   b. See your teacher for clarification.

   Often when teachers announce a test, they will delineate what the test will cover. It can be extremely helpful if they specifically provide a study guide, but often they will not. You certainly can ask if a study guide outlining the things you need to study to be prepared for the test will be available, but often teachers do not provide these. If you have any questions regarding content being covered, *see your teacher for clarification immediately.* Having a clear idea of what your test will cover will inform your study sessions. Sometimes teachers will simply respond with something like, "All of chapter 3." In this case, there are still strategies to help you prepare for the assessments.

   c. Organize notes, handouts, assignments, and any pertinent assessments.

   As soon as a test is announced, organize your notes from class lectures and readings on the topic being tested. Also, organize any handouts you have received from your teacher and any assignments that you have done, along with any quizzes that you have already taken during the unit. If a teacher felt something was important enough for you to do for homework, or important enough to put on a quiz, then there's a good chance you will see it again.

   d. Utilize study guides and practice tests.

Study guides and practice tests are gifts that should never be turned down. If teachers provide a study guide for you, they are essentially telling you what you need to study. They are narrowing the field for you and helping you prepare, providing you do your part. Often teachers (math teachers specifically come to mind) will provide practice tests, or through the online component that often accompanies textbooks, there will be practice tests and quizzes for students to use. These practice assessments are enormously helpful ... if you use them. I have known math teachers who have given practice tests that are exactly like the tests the students will be taking the next day, only they changed the numbers. By utilizing these practice tests early enough, you have the opportunity to see what you already know and what you need to work on. It eliminates surprises. Now it all comes down to you—did you prepare, or didn't you?

e. Create a three- to five-day study plan

Studies support the benefits of distributing study time over several days, versus the same amount of time within fewer days. This is referred to as distributed study versus massed study. Simply stated, what this means to you is that if you plan on studying four hours for an exam, you may be better off spreading the time over two or more nights versus spending four hours the night before.

Depending on how much notice you have had for your test or quiz and also the magnitude of the test or quiz, you might choose to create a three- to five-day study plan. If it is a short quiz and you feel quite comfortable, or if your teacher gives quizzes daily, then obviously you will alter this strategy.

A sample study plan showing when and how you plan to study is shown below.

Study Plan

When	How
Monday—2:45—3:30	See teacher for clarification.
Monday—7:30—8:30	Organize and read through notes.
Tuesday—7:30—8:30	Review chapter questions. Review vocabulary. Take practice test.
Wednesday—2:45—3:30	Review after school with study group.
Wednesday—7:30—8:15	Go over any areas that still need review.

f. Attend review/study sessions.

Many teachers will offer a review/study session prior to a test. Teachers conduct these sessions differently. Some will have their own agenda to follow, reviewing key points and concepts they feel are important; others may be more informal, simply responding to student questions and requests. Either way, teacher-run study sessions can be very helpful, but you need to determine if they are necessary. My recommendation is as always: take a look at your results. If you are testing poorly, see if attending teacher-led review sessions is helpful to you.

If for some reason you know you will be unavailable for the scheduled review session, you can always ask if there is another time your teacher will be available; perhaps before school or even for a few minutes after class may be helpful. When meeting with your teacher, be as specific as possible as to the areas where you need help.

g. Study with other students.

There are a variety of ways that other students can be helpful to you throughout the semester and also as you prepare for tests.

1. Seek out a peer tutor.
    A peer tutor can take several forms; in some high schools, the National Honor Society students offer peer tutoring. This may be done during their study periods or by appointment.

    One of my sons, looking to improve in math during his freshman year, asked an older friend if he would tutor him in exchange for community service hours. Like many schools, his school required a certain number of community service hours, and this proposal created a symbiotic relationship of sorts, where both parties benefited.

2. Study with a fellow student, or in a student study group.
    Studying with students who are taking the same class as you can be beneficial. Other students may have notes that you don't have or may have keyed in to important things you may have missed. You can also test each other and discuss content and concepts together, thus broadening your scope of understanding.

    When working with other students, however, it is a good idea to state your intentions (either to yourself or to your study partner) at the beginning of the session, stating what you hope to accomplish. Your study session must have value. You need to receive something beneficial in exchange for the time you are spending together. If the goals are not clear, it is easy to lapse into unrelated conversation and turn your time into a social visit rather than a work session. Be aware of how you are using your time and hold yourself accountable.

h. Create a study plan checklist.

A study plan checklist is a list of things you're planning to do to prepare for your upcoming assessment. While this checklist may vary depending on the scope and subject matter, it is always a good idea to develop a plan for how you intend to prepare. Below is a sample study plan checklist.

Study Plan Checklist

Activity	Check
Fill in agenda (test date, study dates)	
See teacher for clarification	
Organize notes, hand-outs, and assessments	
Utilize study guides and practice tests	
Create a three- to five-day study plan	
Attend review/study sessions	
Study with other students	
Seek out a peer tutor	

Preparing for Midterms and Finals

Midterm and final exams are the championship games of the testing world. A lot is riding on your performance on these exams. Many of the same strategies and techniques used for studying for tests and quizzes throughout the semester also apply here, especially the part about *keeping up in the first place.*

Midterm and final exams provide a valuable opportunity for you to review and solidify what you have learned over the course of the semester or year. They also count considerably toward your grade for the year. For those reasons, it is well worth preparing for these exams.

Recommendations for preparing for these larger exams are divided into two parts. Part 1 involves preparing for the exams the entire semester, from the moment the semester begins, and Part 2 involves the two or so weeks prior to the actual exams.

Part 1. All Semester Long

a. Save every quiz and test you have taken all semester.
    Your midterm and final exams are cumulative, so it makes sense that material you have been tested on before will appear again. Be sure to correct and understand all errors you made on these assessments as soon as they are handed back to you. If something is still unclear to you, ask your teacher or a classmate for help.

b. Utilize practice tests and quizzes that you have been given or that you have access to.

    Often teachers will give students practice tests ahead of time. Also, depending on the textbook you are using, there is often an e-component that may offer online practice chapter quizzes and tests. Or you might have luck searching for practice problems or practice tests online.

c. Save every study guide your teacher has given you throughout the semester, as these are particularly helpful for review.

    Save important assignments, homework, projects, reports, and labs that you think your teacher may refer to on the test.

d. Pay close attention to and record the things your teacher emphasizes; s/he may specifically preface certain things by saying, "Now this is really important" or "You will definitely be seeing this again."

e. Take good notes during lessons, and keep any notes your teacher may give you. If your teachers hand you something, it is because they feel it is important for you to know.

f. Communicate as soon as possible with your teacher whenever you do not understand something or feel you are falling behind. Too much content is covered in the course of a semester for you to learn it all at the end just for the final exam.

Part 2. Prior to the Midterm or Final

a. Record in your agenda the dates and times of all exams.

b. Set up a study plan. It is never too early to begin reviewing. As you will be studying for more than one subject during midterm and final exams, a study plan is especially important. Your study plan should indicate not only when you plan to study but also what you plan to study for each subject during each study session. Whenever possible, it is best to spread out your studying for each subject over more than one night.

c. Utilize study guides. If you are fortunate enough to be given a study guide, be sure to use it as you are studying. If it is extensive, use it when planning backward in your agenda, seeing how many days it will take you to cover the necessary information and plan accordingly.

d. Attend review sessions. Also, *prepare* for review sessions. Review sessions are much more effective if you have already taken a look at the material and have some specific questions in mind.

e. Check in with your teachers. Seek individual assistance if there are still things you are unsure about or to seek clarification regarding what to study.

f. Organize notes, assignments, labs, and other items that you think you will need, and begin to review.

g. Practice and review past tests and quizzes. The questions on old tests and quizzes were there because your teacher thought they were important for you to know. They could easily appear again.

h. Decide upon study techniques. How will you study for this test? What techniques have worked for you in the past?

i. Develop and utilize a checklist for preparing for midterm and final exams. A sample appears below.

Preparing for Midterm and Final Exams Checklist

Activity	Check
Save every quiz and test you have taken all semester.	
Utilize practice tests.	
Save every study guide you have been given.	
Save important assignments, reports, labs, etc., for review.	
Pay close attention to the things your teacher emphasizes.	
Attend review sessions.	
See your teacher for individual help if needed.	
Organize notes, handouts, assessments, and other materials.	
Practice and review old tests and quizzes.	
Decide upon the study techniques you will use to prepare.	
Set up a three- to five-day study plan.	

Study Techniques

The other component to performing well on tests and quizzes is the actual act of studying, not just setting yourself up to study. What are the different strategies and techniques you can use to study effectively?

Let's start by taking a look at what you currently do when you are studying for a test.

Ways That You Study for a Test

1. _____

2. _____

3. _____

4. _____

Do you always use the same study techniques?

_____

How effective are your methods? Are they equally effective for all subjects? Explain.

_____

Do you analyze your test results and if necessary, change the way you study the next time?

_____

_____

Are there subject areas you would like to improve in? What are they?

_____

Study Techniques

Retrieval Practice

Retrieval practice is a way of holding yourself accountable for your learning while studying. It requires that you recall the information, rather than just recognize it. Retrieval practice is a way for you to actually test yourself as you go along. Without realizing it, many students tend to be too easy on themselves. They think that because they've reviewed something and it is familiar to them, they truly know it. As we mentioned earlier, this involves confusing recognizing material with knowing material.

You can test yourself by seeing what you can produce without the notes or book in front of you and then checking it against your notes or book. In this way, you retrieve what you have learned from your memory, be it the major concepts in a reading selection, mathematical formulas, vocabulary words and definitions, or scientific diagrams. This form of practice has been shown to help solidify the content in your memory. This also forces you to *put the material into your own words*, requiring a higher level of learning and understanding.

Rehearsal

As you begin to learn something for the first time, it is important that you practice something called rehearsal. Rehearsal is the practice of pausing to review and repeat what you have learned, often in your head but also aloud. As an actor might practice or rehearse his or her lines, you are rehearsing what you have learned. Allowing yourself to process and repeat what you have learned will assist you in remembering it later.

An example of this is when you repeat to yourself someone's name you have just met. Peter, Peter, Peter. Peter was prompt and prepared. Here, you've not only repeated it, but you have made a mnemonic connection. Or perhaps when you are trying to memorize a phone number, and you repeat it to yourself a few times until you either chunk the numbers together, or make a little jingle that you are more likely to remember. The oldies song, "867-5309" is a great example of this.

Round up Your Pets or Your Stuffed Animals!—Explaining what you have learned to someone else is a wonderful way to review material and to see how fluent you are with the content. Actually teaching someone else, or pretending to teach (pets or stuffed animals), can help reinforce content and also may shed light on areas that need further review. This is especially helpful when practicing for a presentation or oral report. It can also add a little humor and enjoyment to the study and review process.

Design Your Own Test

As a seventh-grade science teacher, I often had students design their own tests as a homework assignment prior to my unit tests. This was, in a sense, an enforced method of making them study for a test. The tests I received from my students were often both comprehensive and consistent with what I planned to cover. Students included not only the questions but thorough answers too, thus ensuring that they adequately reviewed the material. There was a direct correlation between students designing a thoughtful test and students performing well on the test. Conversely, if a student did not perform well on a test, one of the contributing factors was often that they had not done their "Design Your Own Test" assignment.

At this point in your life, you have been in school for a number of years and have participated in many assessments. As the school year goes on, you will experience the testing styles of your individual teachers. If you think about it, you could probably design the test your teacher is going to give you based on your knowledge of prior tests and the content that has been taught. Depending on the subject matter and your teachers, you will design your tests differently, creating a study experience that is both beneficial and enjoyable.

Designing your own test is an excellent way to review content, hold yourself accountable for material learned, and anticipate and prepare yourself for the actual test.

Vocabulary Study Games

Vocabulary is an integral part of all content areas and forms the foundation for further learning in that subject. Examples of times you will be required to learn vocabulary that is new to you include vocabulary enrichment in English classes, foreign language vocabulary, math and science terms, literary and social science terms, etc.

Many students make and use flash cards for vocabulary study. This is a great idea, as you are creating a way to review, and writing things down can certainly enhance memory, but please remember the difference between recognizing versus knowing the words and definitions. Simply looking at one side of the card and then flipping it over and looking at the back is a good start, but it does not guarantee that you will be able to recall the term or definition later.

Flash Card Games

1.   Using flash cards, you can test yourself or have someone else test you.

2.   Create your own game of memory, also known as concentration. Write all the terms on individual cards. Write all the definitions on another set of cards. Shuffle the cards, and place them all facedown. As you turn them over, match the term with the definition.

3.   Do a simple matching game. Shuffle all definitions and words. Place definitions in one column and words in another. Pair them up, and check for accuracy.

Use A Whiteboard

Having a whiteboard available can be a great addition to your study technique repertoire. Even a small, portable whiteboard will suffice. One way to use a whiteboard when studying new vocabulary is to write the terms on the whiteboard. Then see how many definitions you can write without looking at your notes. Check your answers against your notes. This method is an example of retrieval and holds you accountable for your learning, as you are able to see immediately what you know and what you still need to study. Using a whiteboard also allows you to do something a little different—to use colors and larger muscles, and thus to more actively engage with your learning.

Mnemonics

Utilizing mnemonic strategies is an excellent way to give your memory a boost. Mnemonics take several different forms.

1.   Music—Ever notice how many songs you can sing along to? How did you learn all the words to so many songs? Music can help you remember certain things, particularly lists. I remember teaching my social studies students all the countries of Eastern Europe to the tune of "Camptown Races." My sons were able to recite the fifty states of the United States in alphabetical order by using a song they learned in first grade.

2.   Grouping—Group items on the basis of common characteristics; for example, if you have several foreign language terms you need to remember, you might group them according to meaning or according to structure. Putting items into categories is helpful because there will be fewer categories than items to remember. Once you remember the categories, they will serve as memory cues for the items within them. Now instead of having to memorize twenty random items, you have created four categories with five items of similar characteristics in each one.

3. Names—Name mnemonics are particularly helpful when you need to remember the particular order of something, as in ROY G. BIV, for the colors of the rainbow: red, orange, yellow, green, blue, indigo, violet.

4. Using the First Letters—Also helpful when you need to remember the order of something. Many students have learned the order of the planets using this particular expression: My Very Excellent Mother Just Served Us Nine Pizzas. Mercury, Venus, Earth, Mars, Jupiter, Saturn, Uranus, Neptune, Pluto.

5. Connection Mnemonics—In this case, you are drawing connections between what you need to learn and something you already know. For example; many students struggle with latitude and longitude. Latitude—sounds like ladder—rungs of the ladder go sideways—west to east; Longitude—lines are long—running north to south.

6. Word Games and Word Jingles—I always had difficulty remembering how to spell separate and desperate. I knew one was "ar," and the other "er," but I could never remember which was which. One day someone explained to me how he remembered it. "There's a rat in sep a rat e"—and that was all it took. An example of a well-known word jingle is: Thirty days has September, April, June, and November, all the others have thirty-one, except for February my dear son. It has 28 and that is fine, but in Leap Year, 29.

7. Kinesthetic Mnemonics—This involves using the body or other physical items to trigger memory. Young children often have difficulty differentiating between lowercase b and lowercase d when learning to write. A way to use kinesthetic mnemonics to teach this is to have the kids bring their two fists together, knuckles touching with their thumbs up, representing a bed. The left-hand fist and thumb has made the b, and the right-hand fist and thumb has made the d. I remember instinctively using kinesthetic mnemonics as a child by writing new spelling words in the air.

Utilize Practice Quizzes

Practice quizzes can take many forms, including those mentioned here.

1. Quizlet

   Quizlet is a free website that contains user-generated quizzes, flash cards, and review games on a wide range of topics. You can utilize existing material, or create your own. There are currently in the vicinity of 40 million flash card and study sets.

2. Online sites that accompany your text.

   One example of an online site accompanying a text is the Vocabulary Workshop Series, which has an excellent site to assist in learning and reviewing your vocabulary. Math texts often have online test and quizzes for you to practice that accompany each chapter. Answers are included and explained. If you are not sure if your textbook has an accompanying site, ask your teacher, Google your textbook company, or give them a call.

3. Practice quizzes and tests given to you by your teacher.

   Just like a study guide, if your teacher gives you a practice quiz, start on it right away. That way, if there is something you don't know how to do, you will have time to seek help.

Activate Memory by Addressing Different Learning Styles

Over the years, there has been tremendous focus on different learning styles. It is important to know that although we may favor one style over others, we do not learn by one style alone. Utilizing a variety of learning styles is beneficial to our learning and memory retention. The more ways you can experience information, the more likely you are to retain it. Ways to appeal to various learning styles are listed below.

1. Visual—Access the information visually through reading and writing and utilizing diagrams, charts, and graphs. Use a whiteboard and different-colored markers when studying to visually engage.

2. Auditory—Access the information through hearing and listening, by repeating the information out loud, reading aloud, creating songs, discussing the material with others, and listening to books on tape.

3. Kinesthetic—Access the information physically, by writing either on paper or on a whiteboard, by sense of touch, using manipulatives and models, and by body movement.

   An example of utilizing all three would be learning the parts of a room in a foreign language. Walk around the room, looking at and touching the door, wall, window, etc., while saying the foreign language word for each. Leave sticky notes on the door, wall, window, etc., with the new vocabulary words written on them.

Brain Spill—This study technique requires you to spill everything you know about a given topic, either verbally, or in written form. Afterward, check what you have written against your notes or your textbook to see if it is correct and complete. Using a white board to do this is particularly engaging.

Examples of when to use a brain spill include:

a. Foreign Language—learning the names of furniture; simply imagine yourself in a room, and write down all of the words for what you see in that language. Conjugating verbs.

b. Studying the light and dark reactions of photosynthesis. Can you write down everything you know about these processes? Can you write down the formulas? Afterward, check to see if you are correct and what you're missing.

c. Recalling a timeline of the events leading up to WWII or all the math formulas you might need to know.

d. Recreating diagrams and flow charts that you will need to know.

Reading and Reviewing Notes—It is often helpful to make a photocopy of your notes so one copy can remain untouched and the other can be highlighted or marked up as you go.

Many students like to read their notes out loud, so you are not only seeing your notes, but you're hearing what you're reading also.

Studying with a Study Buddy—This obviously can have advantages and disadvantages. Keep in mind what your goals are for your study session. You want your time to be productive and beneficial, and not turn into a social visit. Schedule time for that afterward. One way to assure your success is to set up a plan with your study buddy before you begin that will address the following:

- What you will study?

- How long you will study?

- How will you study?

Just like when you are working alone, it might help you to build in breaks to help assure that when you are working, you truly are working.

Be Aware of Dwindling Energy—If you feel your attention and focus decreasing, take a short five-minute break. Move your body, have something to eat or drink, get a breath of fresh air, and return to your work.

Preparing for Math Tests and Quizzes

Keeping up in the first place is especially important in courses such as math and foreign language, as so much of what you do will build on what you have previously done. Make sure you pay close attention in class to what is being taught, and seek help as soon as you feel yourself falling behind.

✓ 1.   Practice regularly by doing your nightly homework. In this case, homework is truly practice. The key to understanding and becoming proficient in math is practice and repetition. If there is something in your homework you do not understand, be sure to follow up immediately. Some teachers give full credit simply for doing the assignment. When this happens, students may overlook the fact that there were things they really did not understand.

✓ 2.   Review the questions in your textbook and questions that you've had on previous homework assignments.

✓ 3.   Utilize online quizzes and tests that are offered with your textbook. Often teachers use these as templates for their own tests and quizzes.

✓ 4.   If your teacher provides practice quizzes, seize that opportunity and be sure to do the quiz a minimum of two nights before the test. That way, if you have any difficulties, you still have time to ask your teacher or someone else to explain it to you. Be proactive.

✓ 5.   Memorize specific formulas you may need. Some people assign catchy acronyms to the formulas. One example that comes to mind is "Please excuse my dear Aunt Sally," for order of operations: parenthesis, exponents, multiply, divide, add, subtract. This is a good opportunity to use your white board to see if you can write formulas by heart.

✓ 6.   Just like in other types of tests, be sure to read the directions carefully, marking them up if necessary, and then going back after completing the problem to be sure you have done what you were asked to do. Be sure to answer *all* parts of the question. Too many points in the history of test-taking have been left on the table when a quick moment taken to double check the directions would have made all the difference.

✓ 7. Even if you don't know exactly how to do a math problem, try it anyway. Often as you work through the process, you have an "aha" moment and are able to figure it out. Also, teachers may give partial credit, depending on the problem and circumstances.

✓ 8. Above all, *think* when you are doing your math. Does your answer make sense? Get an idea before you start of what you are looking for. What would be a "ballpark" answer? Estimate.

Test Anxiety

Many students feel they suffer from test anxiety. Common refrains from students are as follows:

"I studied really hard. I just didn't do well."

Or "I knew it when I went in. I just don't know what happened."

So how can that happen? Is it really due to test anxiety? Or could it be something else?

Having a collection of past failures in your repertoire will certainly add to your test anxiety, especially if you're convinced that you studied, knew the material, and still did poorly anyway. Test anxiety is a natural response to the high stakes we place on test grades and performance. Most students experience different levels of anxiety prior to taking a test, and in some cases, having some anxiety can actually increase your performance. But if you feel your test anxiety is what is getting in the way of school success, it is important to address it.

I have found that the best cure for test anxiety is preparation.

The first thing that must be done when addressing test anxiety is to take a look at the way you are preparing for your tests and quizzes. Many students who are putting in adequate study time may need to change *how* they are studying. Many good suggestions for study techniques were found earlier in this book.

The most common suggestion I give to my students is **hold yourself accountable for the content during your studying.**

What does this mean? It means to actually test yourself as you go along. As students review notes, terms, and other things they may be studying, they often inadvertently convince themselves that they are better prepared than they really are. As they review the material, their inner voice may be saying; "Yes, I know that," "Uh, huh, I remember her talking about that," "I remember reading about that," or "Yes, I know these words, I'm all set." In essence, they are *recognizing* the material - it is familiar to them, so they feel comfortable believing that they *know* it.

The question arises – can they recall the information on their own without having it before them? In the case of learning new vocabulary, instead of just reading terms and definitions and thinking you're all set, what I suggest is looking at the term, then without relying on notes or your text, write out the definition on your own. Then check it against the correct answer or response, and actually grade yourself. Also do the reverse. Look at the definitions, and write the term. If you can do this, you *know* the material. You're not really ready for this test until you can actually give yourself a test (written is best) and do well.

I have had students I have worked with actually shake when faced with a test. A contributing factor to this extreme response was, of course, the number of tests they had failed in the past.

The first thing I did with students in this case was simply ask if I could observe them taking their tests in a one-on-one setting. As they worked, I sat quietly at another desk working on something else but still keeping an eye on how they were doing. When they seemed to get stuck, I then intervened. The first thing I needed to determine at this point was, was it test anxiety that prevented them from continuing successfully, or did they not know the material well enough and that contributed to the test anxiety? Let's acknowledge that many students are anxious prior to and even during tests. A lot is riding on your exam grades—they are important. Often students have invested a lot of time and effort into their studying, and it matters deeply to them. Some argue that being a bit nervous or stressed can actually help performance

In just about all cases, the students, who had studied, really did not know the material the way they needed to. They recognized what was being addressed by the test, but were unable to produce the necessary responses from memory alone. This became primarily a studying issue, masked to the student as an anxiety issue. When it became clear that students were not adequately prepared for the exams, we were then able to address study techniques. This served the additional purpose of boosting student confidence as students now felt they had a plan in place. In many cases, they even began to view the test as a contest—them against the test!

While adequate preparation is a major contributing factor in combating test anxiety, there are other strategies that can also be helpful. Try some of these strategies and see how they work for you.

Visualize the test beforehand

Visualize not only the testing environment but also what the test might actually look like. Visualize yourself sitting down in front of the test—scanning through it as you have been instructed, noticing the parts of the test, and estimating how long you will need for each section. Visualize yourself putting your name on the test, and then reading, rereading, and marking up the directions. Picture yourself beginning the test as a calm, test-ready student.

Use relaxation strategies

Practice relaxed breathing—it is very hard to convince your brain that you are stressed when your body is in a relaxed state. Doing deep, yoga-type breaths can assist you in lowering your heart rate and settling you down a bit.

Attitude

Get the right mind-set for the test. Get your game face on. You studied, you prepared, and all that's left is for you is to show up. What will be, will be.

Rely on strategies

People always feel better if they have a plan in place that they can fall back on. Knowing that even if you feel nervous, there are things you know to do can help alleviate anxiety and get you on your way. Remember—you're the student with a plan!

Test-Taking Techniques

Preparing adequately for tests and quizzes is essential, but there's more! You still have to take the test!

This reminds me of the time my husband entered the Monster Dash 10k race dressed as an enormous bunny. Runners typically train and prepare for a race ahead of time—but regardless of their preparation, it all comes down to performance on the day of the race. In the case of the Monster Dash, most of the runners were faster than my husband, so they were well ahead of him at the seven-kilometer mark. Unfortunately, or fortunately for my husband, the lead runner went the wrong way, taking just about everyone else with him! My husband, consulting his map, realized they went the wrong way and proceeded along the correct route, winning the race! What's my message here, you may be asking? Preparation only gets you so far. You can't mess up on the day of the big race, or in your case, the day of the big exam.

What are some things to keep in mind while taking a test?

1. Listen to Directions

Before beginning any test, be sure to listen carefully to all *directions* your teacher or test proctor may be giving you. There could be a last-minute change to the test, an error that needs to be corrected, or other valuable information you might need to know.

Be sure the directions are clear to you—don't hesitate to ask for clarification, either at the beginning of the test, or even during the test if necessary. Your questions are important and have the potential to make a big difference in your test results.

2. Preview the Exam

Once you are allowed to begin the test, *preview* the exam. Get a sense of the layout and different sections of the test by doing a page-turning walkthrough. This should take very little time. While doing this, *estimate the time* you think you will need per section, and then budget accordingly.

3. Read the Directions Twice

Yes, *twice*, and more if necessary. Yes, *twice* and more if necessary. Directions can be very specific and can often be misinterpreted if even a single word is accidentally added or deleted.

4. Mark up the Directions

Feel free to mark up the directions and the test, unless your teacher has told you otherwise.

Actively interact with the directions by underlining or circling key words, such as define, describe, compare, select.

Underline or circle all numbers that you need to pay attention to, like "Give <u>three</u> examples," so that you don't just do one or two.

Practice marking up the following directions:

- Draw a diagram of a plant cell.

- Label at least ten parts.

- Describe three ways a plant cell differs from an animal cell.

- Draw a Venn diagram comparing a plant cell and an animal cell

- Include ten things they have in common

- Include three ways they differ

5.   Skip Questions You Don't Know with a Plan to Return Later

Skip questions that you are stuck on not to use up too much time at the beginning of the test. Mark them (some people put an arrow by the number, some a question mark; it's up to you) so that you don't forget to go back to those questions after you've completed the rest of the test, or if you remember the answer later on during the test.

A common problem for inexperienced test takers, especially those in the lower grades, is to spend so much time on a problem they are having difficulty with that they become overly anxious and run out of time for the rest of the test.

I specifically remember giving the first math test of the year to my third graders. The second question happened to be the most challenging on the test. Even though we had talked about test-taking techniques, if left to their own devices, these inexperienced test takers would have stayed on that question until they got it, in some cases never getting it, thus never moving beyond question 2.

6.   Look over Your Test

When you have completed your test, be sure to look it over completely, looking specifically for items you might have accidentally missed or items you planned to return to. So many students of all ages are just glad to be done with their tests and end up handing in tests that have missing answers, or sometimes even a whole page, that they accidentally overlooked. Had they taken a moment to go back through the test, they would have noticed and done these problems.

Sometimes the test design may be complicated, and while you are working, questions may look like directions and you may skip them. Read *every* word on each page—assume nothing.

7.   Use the Test to Help You

When you do skip a question, or answer a question but are unsure, keep a watchful eye and a keen mind as you progress through the rest of the test. Often answers to questions are actually used in other test questions, or other questions may trigger your thought processes and move you on to realizing an answer to a question.

Recently a student was taking a test that was organized into six sections, with section titles. The final question was to cite six key elements and to describe them in detail. The student was able to recall four of the elements and then sat wracking her brain for the other two. Toward the end of the test, as she looked it over for the final time, she realized the six headings were, in fact, the six parts she was looking for, and bingo, she was on her way.

Specific Strategies for Specific Types of Tests

During your school career, you will encounter many different types of tests. Matching the type of test you are taking with effective strategies will be very beneficial. Multiple choice questions and essay questions are commonly used on assessments.

Multiple Choice Questions

1.   Read the question twice.

     Even if you think you understand it, read the question twice just to be sure you haven't misread anything. Read it again if you need to.

2.   Use the cover up method.

     As you read the question, cover the answers and see what your brain is thinking. What do you think is the answer?

3. Read *all* of the choices.

    See if what you were thinking is one of the choices, but be sure to read them all anyway. You may be thinking during the cover-up method of one answer, and then see as you read the choices that a better answer is offered.

4. Choose the best answer.

    If you are not absolutely sure what the answer is after trying the cover-up method and reading all the choices, try solving by the process of elimination. Get rid of the choices you know are wrong. When you do that, at least you increase your chances of being correct.

5. Pay attention to specific words.

    Watch out for words such as always, never, only, and all of the above, as they will require further thought.

6. Use contextual clues.

    Often, just like locating answers in a test, clues to the answer may be in the question. Using contextual clues found in the question may help you figure out the answer, as in the following question.

Sample Multiple Choice Question

The cumbersome camera equipment made it difficult for the photographer to squeeze through the opening to get a good photo. The word *cumbersome* is best defined as:

A. Crude

B. Unwieldy

C. Unprotected

D. Slow-moving

The contextual clue contained in this sentence is that the camera equipment made it difficult to squeeze through an opening, giving the impression that it is large and awkward; unwieldy.

Essay Questions

Essay questions appear frequently on assessments. In order to be successful with essay questions, it is important to be proactive, meaning there are valuable things you can do before you even start.

Preparing before Test Day

In many instances, essay questions can be prepared for prior to test day. If you have any idea what essay questions your teacher is likely to ask, you can prepare ahead of time by creating an outline, making a list of key points to address, or actually practicing writing out the essay. Often a teacher may indicate in class likely essay topics or questions that will appear on the test, or they might even include them in a study guide. As you become more familiar with your teachers and the types of questions they ask, you will become more adept at predicting what will be asked of you. If your teacher tells you ahead of time what the essay will be, or even gives you a general idea, there is no reason not to make good use of this valuable information.

One example I can give of this is when I took my comprehensive exam for my master's degree. I knew ahead of time that this exam would consist of six essay questions that needed to be addressed in depth and detail. The question was, what would those essay questions be? After reviewing my notes in the separate binders that I kept for each class, I made an educated guess as to what would be asked of me. For the month prior to the exam, I prepared for and practiced writing these essays and was on the mark for the exam.

Before Starting to Write

1.   Read and Mark Directions Carefully

As in all directions, read the essay question(s) twice, and mark up important information to be sure you answer the questions correctly and completely.

Practice marking up the following directions:

Describe three challenges Germany faced when invading Russia and how they affected the outcome of the war.

Explain how the climate and geography of a region relate to the economics of a region. Cite and describe three specific examples.

2. Budget Your Time

If there is more than one essay, be sure to budget your time accordingly. If you have one hour and two essays to write, plan to allot approximately thirty minutes per essay. You may want to actually take your watch off your wrist and place it on your desk so you can continually monitor your time.

3. Prewriting Strategies

Sometimes, getting started may be a challenge. Here are some ideas that might help.

a. Do a quick brainstorm—quickly jot down the things that come to mind that you want to be sure to include before starting.

b. Utilize graphic organizers—templates follow:

- A very simple graphic organizer involves placing the topic in a circle in the center of a piece of scrap paper. Draw three or more lines radiating out from the center of the circle to surrounding circles. In those circles, place key points you want to address. If necessary, you can draw additional radiating lines from those circles and include specific details you might want to include.

- Another type of graphic organizer is helpful for planning a five-paragraph essay. This graphic organizer shows five blocks for the five paragraphs you will write. Block 1 (paragraph 1) = introduction with thesis statement, blocks 2, 3, and 4 (paragraphs 2, 3, 4) = ideas to develop, and block 5 (paragraph 5) = the conclusion.

- If the essay involves a compare and contrast question, you might want to utilize a Venn diagram and quickly jot in the appropriate places the key things you want to address.

- Use your graphic organizers as a guide, knowing that additional things may develop as you progress through your essay.

4. Wrapping up

If time allows, proofread your essay for clarity and mechanics, such as spelling, grammar, and word choice.

Sample Graphic Organizers:

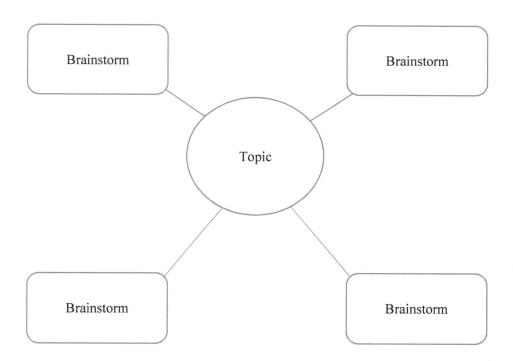

5 Paragraph Essay – Graphic Organizer

Paragraph 1 - Introduction –Thesis statement and supporting points

Paragraph 2 – Body Paragraph

Paragraph 3 – Body Paragraph

Paragraph 4 – Body Paragraph

Conclusion

7
Reading Assignments

A major component of your educational experience in high school, in college, and for the rest of your life, involves independent reading—the reading you do on your own to gain information and increase your personal knowledge.

> If one reads enough books one has a fighting chance. Or better, one's chances of survival increase with each book one reads.
> — Sherman Alexie

What does this quote mean to you?

_____

_____

_____

_____

Reread it again if you have to, but don't go on until you have an answer.

To me, it's all about the first point made in The Three Big Reasons to Do Well: Everything You Learn You Get to Take With You. Reading has the ability to enhance your life, to make you stronger. You've heard the saying, "Knowledge is power." Readers make themselves available to an endless source of knowledge, but they have to read to do this.

While it is ideal to view your education as a shared responsibility between you and your teacher, as you progress through the grades, this responsibility falls more and more on your shoulders. Much of the education takes place in the classroom, but much also takes place through you and your interaction with the assigned reading. In fact, that is where so much of your individual processing and absorption takes place.

Students who do not do the readings, or look for a shortcut, gain far less from their experiences than those who delve deeply into the reading. Remember the reason you are here—you get to take it with you. If you don't read it, you don't take it with you, and by the end of the semester, you've still spent the same amount of time in the class; the only difference is while others have been reading and benefitting and preparing to take all they learn with them, you have looked for a shortcut and gained very little. You may also find yourself more anxious and worried about how you are going to do on the exams because you are missing the greater understanding that comes from doing the reading. You now become more concerned with your grade than you are with what you have learned and have lost sight as to what that grade actually means. Are you someone who just passed the time somewhere, or are you someone who is coming away with more than you had when you started?

A common mistake that students make is that they don't give reading assignments their due. Yes, a reading assignment *is* homework. But because it often is not assigned with a writing assignment or something tangible to hand in the next day, the tendency might be to not treat it with the same seriousness. But reading is truly the crux of your education, a major contributor to all you will learn. If you take shortcuts with your reading assignments, you are also shortening all you will learn. This will show in your results—not just on assessments, but in what you will know as a person when you get out of school.

In a survey, when college freshmen were asked if they felt they were prepared for their college experience, many responded by saying that they wished they had read more in high school. The amount of independent reading you will have in college is almost certain to increase. How will you manage those increased demands if you have not *practiced* in high school? High school is a place to practice your reading stamina—your ability to stick with a challenging reading selection, and see it through to completion. Remember the third point in The Three Big Reasons to Do Well: You're Practicing the Skills You Need to be Successful.

Reading requires stamina, and stamina requires practice.

How to Approach Assigned Reading

Has this ever happened to you?

You've just finished reading the whole page and have no idea what you've read? I'm guessing you're nodding your head and saying, "Yes, it has." Having no idea what you just read is not going to help you at all. If you are reading the words but your mind is elsewhere, or if you are reading and decoding the words accurately, but they just seem to bounce off your face without penetrating into a place of thought and comprehension, then that is as good as not reading at all.

In order for you to get the most out of your reading assignments, you must *monitor your understanding* as you read. Don't wait until you're done with the page or chapter to note that you haven't absorbed a thing. Learn to check your engagement and monitor your comprehension as you go along.

There are numerous strategies you can implement that will keep you more engaged with the text and help you understand what you have read. When you implement these strategies, you become what is known as an *active reader*. In essence, you are *thinking* while you are reading. You are thinking about *what* you are reading.

Effective Reading Strategies

1. Be Aware of Your Inner Voice

Effective readers are thinking about what they are reading as they are reading. For many, this takes the form of an inner voice that is continually interacting with the material. It is the voice that is saying things like, "Whoa, I better read that again, didn't quite get it the first time," or "I didn't see that coming," or "I know who did it! Can't fool me!" or "My grandfather lived through that war. I wonder where he was at that time."

While effective readers are reading, they actively make connections to things they already know, build on prior knowledge, formulate questions, make predictions, draw inferences, synthesize information, visualize what is happening as if in a movie scene, and a host of other comprehension strategies.

If your inner voice is responding to what you are reading, then you are actively reading. If your inner voice is not there, then you're not there!

2. Preview the Reading Material

Especially in the case of nonfiction material, effective readers preview the reading material. They do this by scanning the chapter before reading, looking at headings, subheadings, diagrams, illustrations, focus questions, and vocabulary. By previewing the reading material, you are priming your brain for what is to come.

3. Be Aware of Your Attention Span

After previewing the material, it is often helpful to divide the reading into manageable sections. Knowing there is a predetermined break, perhaps after thirty minutes or after the first section, can help keep you focused. If you are aware of your attention span waning, meaning you can no longer hear that inner voice, it is time to take a break—perhaps get a drink of water, or have a movement break. Remember, it serves no purpose to just read the words and not have any idea what you have read.

4. Interact with the Text

Along with actively thinking about what you are reading, an additional strategy is to physically interact with the text. This is done by marking or annotating while you are reading. Readers do this in a variety of ways, including using a highlighter to highlight important information, jotting notes in margins, jotting notes on sticky notes, and writing brief summaries at the end of sections. Often having a pencil in hand and assigning an active task while reading serves to hold the readers more accountable and keeps them more involved.

5. Understand Different Forms of Text

Different forms of texts will require different strategies. Below are two strategies that are especially useful for monitoring your understanding while reading nonfiction texts, such as a science or history text. The more you practice these techniques, the more likely you are to incorporate them seamlessly into reading practices.

RCRC—Read, Cover, Recite, Check

Read—a paragraph, passage, or section

Cover—the paragraph with your hand or index card

Recite—back what you have read; key points, important details, etc.

Check—uncover the paragraph and check.

(Archer and Gleason, 1989)

SQ3R—Survey, Question, Read, Recite, Review

Survey (prime the brain for the task at hand): Preview the reading selection noticing headings, subheadings, graphics, vocabulary, key questions, focus points, etc.

Question (focus and engage the reader): Prior to reading each section, turn the section heading into a focus question for you to concentrate on as you read. Example: A subheading stating, "Characteristics of All Living Things" can be changed into a focus reading question of, "What are the characteristics of all living things?"

Read (gather information): Reading one section at a time, be aware of your inner voice. Focus on the question you have in mind. Were there other things addressed in the selection?

Recite (hold yourself accountable—a concentration exercise): After each section, see if you can recall your question and answer it from memory. If not, go back, check the selection, and try again.

Review (organize and build memory): Review what you have learned from the selection, using headings and subheadings as your guide. Can you explain what you have just read? What have you learned here that's new?

(Robinson, 1946)

6. Monitor Comprehension

Keeping track of your understanding as you read is essential, especially as content becomes lengthier and more complex. Your inner voice can help you with this and serves as your first line of defense. If you notice your inner conversation has gone from, "Oh, I see," and "That's so interesting" to "I don't get this" and "What? I don't remember learning about that," it is time to put the brakes on and implement some additional comprehension strategies.

    a. Identify what you don't understand.

    b. Reread the passage.

    c. Adjust your reading speed to allow for better comprehension.

    d. Pause and reflect at the end of each section.

    e. Summarize what you have learned, noting main ideas and supporting details.

f. Take notes in margins or on a separate piece of paper. Read with a pencil in your hand.

g. Restate what you have just read in your own words.

h. Pretend to teach someone the material.

i. iHold yourself accountable for what you have read.

Remember—Reading Takes Time

Allow yourself ample time for reading assignments when you are planning your evening or weekly work schedule. You are much more likely to enjoy what you are reading and to process what you are reading if you are not pressured by time or too tired because you saved it for the last minute. Give yourself the "gift of time" for your reading assignments, and it will be both pleasurable and beneficial.

8

Facing down Obstacles

Challenges and difficulties are bound to come up during your school year. Can you think of some things that might present an obstacle to your school success?

1. _____

2. _____

3. _____

Students I have worked with have cited things like illness, playing sports, a part-time job, driver's ed, girlfriends/boyfriends, a change in family or living situation, a particular weakness in a subject area, and a teacher they don't get along with, among others.

Chances are that there is no one, and never has there been anyone, who has made it through four years of high school without ever facing any obstacles. Obstacles are just a part of the obstacle course of life. They're there, and sometimes they even serve a beneficial purpose. The good news in school is that you're not in this alone. When students have come to me discouraged, fearful that they may not succeed, I let them in on a little secret that they probably aren't aware of. I tell them, "This school is here for *you*. Yes, *you*. Without *you*, there is no reason for this school to even exist. Your teachers are here for you, the principal is here for you; your success is what we are all about. So if you are having difficulty, make your teacher a partner in your success."

Be Your Own Advocate

I know that many students are hesitant for one reason or another to approach a teacher for extra help. But it has been my experience that when a student candidly sits down with a teacher and says, "I don't understand this. Do you think you can help me?" most teachers are more than happy to oblige. Teaching you is the reason they are there in the first place. The other important lesson that is learned here is to advocate for yourself. By advocating for yourself, I mean asking for help when you need it, speaking up for yourself in order to help yourself succeed. This does not mean that you sit in class, utterly inattentive, or chatting with a friend during class time and then expect your teacher to give you a one-on-one lesson later. It means you're putting in an honest effort to learn and expecting your teacher to put in an honest effort to teach you.

A former student came back to visit me from college and recounted this story regarding an upper-level math course he was struggling with. He went for help during his math professor's office hours. Upon reviewing his recent test grades (he had struggled with the content), the professor did not wish to assist him as he felt the student was not putting the necessary effort into his work and was simply worried about his grade. The student replied, "You don't understand. I'm not asking you to do anything about my grade. I just want to be sure I learn this material. I'm going to need this when I get out of school and I need a little more help understanding it." The professor took a good look at him and responded, "Have a seat. Let's get started."

Acknowledging that there will be obstacles is one thing, but how do you prevent them from derailing you in your quest to be a successful student?

First of all, you have to know that they will happen. Period. Obstacles will be coming your way. If they haven't already, don't worry, they're coming. If they have already come your way, then hopefully they have made you stronger—you have learned to succeed despite them. As obstacles arise, you have an opportunity to practice developing strategies to solve problems.

Second, keep in mind Key Element 3—Be Your Own Cheerleader—and develop an inner voice that is supportive and encouraging and leads you to look for strategies.

When your inner voice is saying something like, "Oh no, not again," or "I didn't see that coming," or "This is not good," have an inner voice that responds with something like, "So, what now? What are some of the things I can do to help myself? What's my plan? Who can I ask to help me? What must I do?"

Since you have been learning to continuously evaluate your progress and to tweak your efforts along the way to better match the situation, you will apply that skill to your new problems. An illness that has kept you out of school for five days and left you with what looks like an insurmountable amount of work can be faced with a plan that looks like this:

1. On the first day back, see all of my teachers and find out what I missed.

2. Set up a schedule for the work that needs to be made up.

3. Prioritize the work.

4. Keep up with all new work while chipping away at the missed work.

Choose from the following situations.

Situation 1: The semester just began two weeks ago, and I already feel behind. I just don't get what we're doing. Algebra 1 was difficult for me; how will I survive Algebra 2?

Situation 2: Hockey (or insert another sport/activity) is starting. With practices, games, and traveling back and forth to the ice rinks/fields, how will I ever get all my work done?

Situation 3: Uh-oh. Another research paper. Long-term projects are my nemesis. I hope this isn't going to be one more nightmare.

What is the problem?

_____

_____

_____

_____

Brainstorm solutions/strategies:

1. _____

2. _____

3. _____

4. _____

What will you do first, and when will you do it?

1. _____

2. _____

3. _____

4. _____

Monitor your progress.

_____

_____

_____

_____

Have you seen positive results?

_____

_____

_____

_____

Are additional changes necessary? If so, repeat the process and/or ask a teacher, peer, or educational professional to assist you in the process.

An example of what a problem-solving strategy worksheet looks like for Situation 1 follows.

What is the problem?

I feel lost in Algebra 2. I don't get what we're doing, and I'm afraid I will struggle like I did with Algebra 1.

Brainstorm solutions/strategies

1. See my teacher for help.

2. Ask my older brother to explain it to me.

3. Increase the time I spend at home on math.

4. Make my own practice quizzes.

What will you do first, and when will you do it?

1. I will ask my teacher when she is available for help.
   When: Today after class

2. I will ask my brother if he is willing to set up a regular time with me to study math.
   When: This evening after dinner

3. I will be sure to put time aside every single school day for math.
   When: I will start today.

4. Make my own practice quizzes.
   When: On weekends, I will review what we have learned that week and make up a quiz in the same format that my teacher does.

Problem-Solving Strategy Worksheet

(Use as obstacles arise.)

What is the problem?

_____

_____

Brainstorm solutions/strategies

    1. _____

    2. _____

    3. _____

    4. _____

What will you do first, and when will you do it?

    1. _____

    2. _____

    3. _____

    4. _____

Monitor your progress.

_____

_____

Have you seen positive results?

_____

_____

Are additional changes necessary? If so, repeat the process and/or ask a teacher, peer, or educational professional to assist you in the process.

This problem-solving strategy technique can also be applied to repeating daily problems like the following:

Not doing homework

Not completing homework

Missing deadlines

Not using an agenda

Forgetting necessary materials (either at school or at home)

Procrastinating

Not putting in sufficient study time

Disorganized binders, backpacks, workspaces, etc.

Becoming distracted while working

And most other problems and challenges you may encounter.

9

Evaluating Your Progress

Success is not a one-and-done thing. You don't achieve it and then sit back for the rest of your life as a success. The same thing can be said for failure. Neither is permanent.

As you progress through your school year(s), it's essential that you monitor your progress and frequently evaluate how things are going for you.

Is what you're doing working for you? If you're not sure, think of the following.

It is extremely easy to know if things are working for you in a school setting as the proof is in the pudding, as they say. Just look at your results, and in school that means your grades. School provides a steady, in fact daily, stream of feedback. That feedback comes in the form of grades on homework, projects, participation, assessments, and also in the form of teacher and parent approval and in self-satisfaction. You know immediately when something has gone well, and you know immediately when it could have gone better. What you do with that feedback is what matters.

Skilled students continuously think about what they are doing, and whether it is yielding the results they are looking for. As time goes on, you will notice that you also are doing this quite naturally, and actually all the time. Consider the following examples.

Scenario 1

You receive a 65 percent on a quiz. You're not happy about this score, but as you think about it, you realize you're not really surprised. You didn't begin studying for this quiz until the night before, and you weren't able to see the teacher for clarification on things you weren't sure about prior to the quiz as you had planned. You compare that with the two quizzes you had taken earlier in the quarter. In both those instances, you earned solid Bs. "Well," you say to yourself, "I did begin studying earlier, and I had time to see the teacher for help, and that certainly seemed to make a difference."

Moral of the story—if I want to do well on the next quiz, I better start studying earlier and leave myself time to see my teacher if necessary.

Scenario 2

You've studied for a test and feel well prepared and fairly confident. As you begin your test, you realize there's an entire section covering something you weren't expecting. You do your best but know that this is going to dramatically affect your score. This is too bad, because had you known this was going to be on the test, you certainly would have reviewed the material. "Well," you say to yourself, "I'm not going to let that happen again. Next time, as soon as a test is announced, I'm going to confirm with the teacher exactly what will be covered so I can better prepare myself."

Scenario 3

Yes! I finally did well on a chemistry test. For the first time ever, I earned above a C. Yup, it looks like the three-day study plan really helped. I am definitely going to do that again!

What have I been doing that has been working for me?

Do I need to be doing something differently?

Simply asking yourself these and other related questions can serve as a navigational beacon for your school journey. Am I on the right path, or do I need to make some changes?

I recently met with an honors math student to discuss his very low first-quarter grade. As he and I took a careful look through all of his quiz and test scores for the quarter, we noticed how consistent they were. All five scores, which were earned over a two-month span, were in the low sixties. Our conversation went something like this;

Me—I see your test and quiz scores are really consistent.

Student—Yeah, consistently bad.

Me—Were you happy with any of them?

Student—No, not a single one.

Me—So what did you do after you received the first low test grade?

Student—What do you mean?

Me—Did you change the way you prepared for the next test? Or change how you did anything else?

Student—Not really.

Me—So here's what I've found over the years. If you want something to change, you have to change what you are doing.

What are some things you might do differently to get different results?

A thinking student takes a look at what is going on and makes changes as necessary, just as a driver makes adjustments to the road he or she is driving on with each bend and hill that he or she encounters.

What follows are forms I use with my students at the beginning of a new quarter and at the end of semester one to help them evaluate their progress and consider changes that might be beneficial.

Starting a New Quarter

1. What worked well for you last quarter? What do you want to keep doing?

    _____

    _____

    _____

    _____

2. What were your grades?

    Subject and grade   Satisfied—Yes/No

    _____   _____

    _____   _____

    _____   _____

    _____   _____

    _____   _____

    _____   _____

3. What are you thinking of doing differently? How will you do it?

    _____

    _____

    _____

    _____

Setting up for Semester 2

1. What worked well for you in semester 1?

    _____

    _____

    _____

    _____

2. What were your grades?

Subject and grade	Midterm Exam	Satisfied – Yes/No
_____	_____	_____
_____	_____	_____
_____	_____	_____
_____	_____	_____
_____	_____	_____

3. What are you thinking of doing differently? How will you do it?

    _____

    _____

    _____

    _____

Now That I'm up and Running, How Do I Stay in the Game?

You've been working hard, implementing strategies and making necessary changes, and things are going well. You're well organized and well prepared, and your grades are strong. How do you keep this good thing going? One thing to keep in mind is that if what you are doing is working, keep doing it! Often students make changes, begin to see improvement, and then revert back to earlier habits. If it is working, keep doing it. If it is not, critically analyze and make some changes until it does work.

Think of the top athletes you know. What are the things that they do to stay in the game? They hustle, they watch out for obstacles, they make adjustments as needed, and they are in it for the entire game. In sports, when you hustle, you move or act intentionally and energetically to work toward your goal. The same goes for school. You hustle by doing the things we have been talking about—by purposefully taking care of your responsibilities. You don't let opportunities for success pass you by, and you don't come up short in the effort and commitment department.

The road to success is not an easy one. As the saying goes, ***if it wasn't hard, everyone would do it.***

Part of succeeding is expecting to have challenging times. Yes, there will also be lots of easy, smooth-sailing times, but if you acknowledge there will be challenging times, you will be better able to successfully work through them. There will be times when you *will* be challenged, you *will* be tired, and you *will* question your ability to succeed. These challenges, experienced and overcome, raise you to the next level and give you a feeling of deep satisfaction.

You can't climb the mountain by walking on level ground.

Ultimately, what you do in school is up to you. Your parents may want you to be successful, your teachers may want you to be successful, but when all is said and done, it is you who will either work or not. It is you who will determine how much you grow and how much you gain during your days and years in school. Although there will be others who will try to determine this for you through external motivation, like praise and various rewards, studies show that your best and longest-lasting motivation will come from internal factors, like the feeling you get when you've worked hard on something and given it your best. Your motivation will come from knowing the reasons why you are working hard and knowing how your life will be enriched by doing well. Your motivation will come from frequently revisiting The Three Big Reasons to Do Well:

- You get to take all you learn with you.

- It increases your options and makes you more marketable.

- You are practicing the skills you need to be successful in school and beyond.

Yes, occasionally motivation is sure to wane, but if you remind yourself why it is important for you to do well, you will be much more likely to overcome periods when you are less motivated than others. Remind yourself of why you want to succeed, what you hope to do with your life, and how good it will feel to achieve these goals. And keep in mind that what you do today is practice—practice for tomorrow, practice for next year, and practice for the rest of your life.